Pirates

Written by Marjorie Newman
Illustrated by Phil Garner

Collins Educational
An Imprint of HarperCollinsPublishers

When you have found his
clothes, turn the page.

When you have found
the food beginning
with **b**, turn the page.

very deep

more Sharks

even deeper

Treasure Island

buried treasure

y hidden rocks

bosuns bridge

swamp island

whirlpools

jelly fish island

N
W
E
S

When you have given the directions, turn the page.

When you have found the rhyming pairs, turn the page.

Treasure Island keep off

When you have found a safe way to get to the land, turn the page.

When you have worked out what
is inside the chest, turn the page.

HOME ENTERTAINMENT

DISCOVERIES AND INVENTIONS

Rodney Dale
Rebecca Weaver

THE BRITISH LIBRARY

Inside front cover   A rebus
Page 1   'Dressing the doll', 1901
Pages 2 and 3   Wallis's game – see page 13

Photographic acknowledgements
All illustrations in this book have been taken from
out-of-copyright material in the British Library's collections
with the exception of those which carry a credit line in the
accompanying caption. Patents are numbered and dated for
ease of reference.

©1993 Rodney Dale and Rebecca Weaver

First published 1993 by
The British Library, Great Russell Street,
London WC1B 3DG

British Library Cataloguing
In Publication Data
is available from The British Library

ISBN 0 7123 0301 4

Designed by Roger Davies.
Set in Palatino on Ventura.
Printed in Italy.

Contents

Home Amusements

R CAMDEN

Introduction

We may divide the whole struggle of the human race into two chapters: first the fight to get leisure; and then the second – what shall we do with our leisure when we get it?
James A Garfield, in an address at the Chautauqua Institution, New York State, 1880.

Today in advanced industrialized nations there is barely enough work to go round and James Garfield's 'fight' has almost been turned on its head – in the face of less or no work we are clinging on desperately to what work we have. Leisure time doesn't hang naturally on most of us. The 'leisured classes' have indeed been lucky – lucky to be able to cope with all that leisure time.

Leisure never presented a problem to the gentry and upper classes; there were always activities associated with land owning and a tradition of not-always-amateur dabbling in the civilised arts.

From 1850 large numbers of working people – both skilled and those working in officially-inspected places – worked a 60-hour week. From 1874 they were granted a half-day on Saturdays and four statutory bank holidays a year. This legislation precluded all rural workers, shopworkers and those myriads of artisans – for example toy-makers and less-skilled workers engaged in sewing, match-making, and box making – to say nothing of those in domestic service. Statistically, Americans worked longer, their week not dropping from the mid-century 70 hours to 60 hours until about 1900.

To this extent, then, 'leisure' has denoted a certain gentility associated with the next rung up the social ladder. It is interesting to note that 'working class' entertainment has always been characterized as a sociable, gregarious, veritably vulgar entertainment, whereas the middle classes have exuded a discipline and restraint and seriousness of purpose, a privacy which has nonetheless had its aspiring numbers. Having obtained leisure, the problem was to know what to

A New England Fireside – *Ballou's Pictorial* **10 March 1855.**

Horse Exercise at Home.

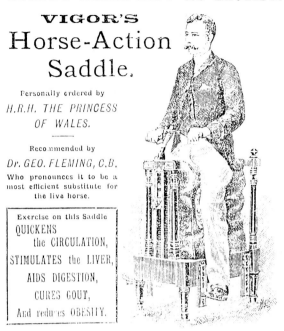

An advertisement in *Knowledge* – 1 November 1895.

do with it. The *Saturday Review* admitted (4 June 1870): 'We really do not know how to amuse ourselves' – speaking for the orderly middles classes, of course, and their 'weary hours of sobriety'.

As affluence moved down the social scale, increased numbers of people were moving into the new suburbias mushrooming in every town. These new houses boasted a gas (and later electricity) supply which enabled the occupants to extend their days artificially well beyond sunset. Artificial light was – and is, though we now take it for granted – crucial in broadening the scope in many homes for leisure activities. The improving Englishman was indeed acquiring his castle. For the working classes left in tenements and single rooms it was a question of 'Leisure? – What leisure?' Going to the pub was still the most popular release from the pressures of life. Children from these homes were shunted outside and their ubiquitous presence is later remarked upon. That children should

be seen and not heard had, from a middle-class standpoint, a utilitarian as well as a disciplinarian motive; indeed the contributor to 'The Gatherer' section of *Cassell's Magazine* in 1890 is full of praise for 'Seven new games for children that do not involve constant shouting.' Cassell's compendium quoted below was not for boys of this class.

Incidental information about contemporary habits can be gleaned from most works of fiction – from Jane Austen, through Willa Cather, Edith Wharton to D H Lawrence – but two works afford particularly amusing insights. *The Diary of a Nobody* (George and Weedon Grossmith) was published serially in Punch in 1888–9, and has been in print ever since. The 'Nobody' is Mr Charles Pooter, an unpretentious clerk in the City, who is inspired to write a diary when he and his wife Carrie move into their new suburban house. For the Pooters, it has been satisfying enough to acquire this sort of house: aspirations to notions of profitable home entertainment will wait:

Carrie and I can manage to pass our evenings without friends and there is always something to be done: a tin-tack here, a Venetian blind to put straight, a fan to nail up or part of a carpet to nail down all of which I can do with a pipe in my mouth. Carrie is not above putting a button on a shirt, mending a pillow-case, or practising the 'Sylvia Gavotte' on our new cottage piano (on the three years' system).

The other source of illumination is a collection of stories now known as *The Eliza Stories* by Barry Pain. These were five short books, the first of which was published in 1900, depicting scenes from the suburban-villa life of another city clerk and his long suffering wife Eliza. Eliza spends virtually all her evenings sewing – sewing of the useful necessary kind. Her husband attempts to divert her, trying to foster an interest in books which he occasionally reads aloud, but she is unyielding in her attachment to her needle.

Both books reveal the basic banality of home entertainment for the vast majority of people. The market for anything other than card games, pianos on the instalment plan, the mandatory sewing, books – and, of course, newspapers – was restricted to those with a more deeply-rooted educational background and with lots more money.

As we shall see, unbridled amusement and fun was enough to raise the eyebrows of several sections of the community – intellectual notions of live and let live

Examples of the high art of fretwork. The fretsaw was usually operated by hand; the afficionado would use a treadle-operated machine, as illustrated on page 50.

never seem to work in practice. Yet the growing sciences of psychology and psychiatry around the turn of the century were beginning to suggest that enjoyable leisure time was in fact rather healthy and should be encouraged. This theory coincided with the maturing idea that the family was a good thing and that family spirit and happiness should also be encouraged. This was at a time when many women were finding that machines in the home were reducing the time needed for their daily chores. So social theory, science, technology and not a little money have, throughout the 20th century, led advertisers to promote their amusement, games and toys as 'fun for all the family'. Nowadays there has been a further shift; leisure activities are for simple self-fulfilment.

There was always the stated middle-class fear that increasing leisure would undermine the discipline of their world, offering an invitation to indolence. Pleasure was indeed a legitimate part of life – but not a legitimate end in itself. In America at least, taking up hobbies was actively encouraged. A hobby was perceived as having moral value and fostering serenity; it was purposeful pursuit.

Collecting, as a hobby, was more associated with the upper and educated classes – collecting 'valuables' such as books, coins, stamps, works of art, and clocks; and collecting natural history specimens, such as fossils, shells, insects, and butterflies. Some of these activities were more open to the less affluent than others – collecting shells and insects gradually became popular in the 1880s for instance. As means have grown, collecting has become a favourite hobby with many and the range of collectibles is legion.

The pursuit of a skill, a craft or a sport is a recognition that energies are not solely required as a means of production, nor as support for a dependent family. The range of skills, crafts and sports to which working-class people turned their attention is revealed by the significant growth of 'special interest' journals in the 1890s. Many, indeed most, crafts were not new – beadwork, fretwork, and crochet, for example – but the seriousness of the devotion of energy and time to them was. Outdoors, organized sport and exercising was a commendable way to harness excess energy and many athletics, cycling, tennis and other sports clubs date from the end of the 19th century. It was easier to communicate, people were going out and about more, there was more confidence, more affluence, and more time. As the 20th century moved on, developments such as aeronautics, motor cars and wireless – soon to become radio – were embraced with unquestioning enthusiasm.

'The Celebrated "Miss Plankfirst" the Dancing Suffragette'. Topicality and ingenuity, a combination behind many successful toys.

'The advantages of gymnastics for the young are incontestable, but practically there are difficulties in the way, particularly for those living in the towns, but a skilful American has solved the problem in an ingenious way.'

"HOW DO YOU LIKE YOUR NEIGHBOUR?"

The company must seat themselves round the room, leaving plenty of space in the middle for passing to and fro. One person left standing then begins the game by putting the question, "How do you like your neighbour?" to any one he pleases. The answer must be either "Not at all" or "Very much." Should the reply be "Not at all," the lady or gentleman is requested to say what other two members of the company would be preferred instead as neighbours, when the new neighbours and the old must immediately change places. During the transition the questioner may endeavour to secure a seat for himself, leaving out one of the four who have been struggling for seats to take the place of questioner. When the reply "Very much" is given, every one in the room must change places. The questioner, therefore, will easily find a seat for himself, and the person left standing must take his place as interrogator.

"HOW, WHEN, AND WHERE?"

In this game, like the last, a word is chosen by the company, containing as many meanings as possible, the person who has volunteered to be the questioner having previously gone out of the room. On being recalled, the person who has been out begins by asking each of his friends how they like it.

Supposing the word "cord" to have been chosen, the first player might answer *slight*, the next *sweet*, meaning *chord*, the next *loud*, the next *strong*, and so on until all have said *how* they liked it. The questioner then recommences his interrogations at the first player by inquiring "*When* do you like it?" Replies to this question something like the following may be given:— "When I am preparing to take a journey;" "When I am in church;" "When I am driving;" "When I feel musical." Then to the last question—"Where do you like it?" the company may reply—"In a piano;" "In the garden;" "Not round my neck;" "Always at hand," &c. No doubt long before all the questions have been answered the word that has been chosen will have been discovered.

HUNT THE RING.

The game of Hunt the Ring is perhaps better liked than Hunt the Slipper, on account of its being in the estimation of most people more convenient and manageable. Either a ring or a small key may be used for the purpose. Whichever it is, a string must be passed through it, and the ends fastened in a knot, forming thus a circular band. The company then stand in a circle, allowing the string to pass through the hands of each person, and enabling every one to slide the ring easily along from one to the other. The object of the player standing inside the circle is to stop it in its progress, which, in most cases, he finds a rather difficult task. The game is also frequently played without any string, when every one tries, of course, to pass the ring round very rapidly, without being detected by the hunter.

HUNT THE SLIPPER.

This surely must be one of our oldest games, and one, no doubt, that our grandmothers and grandfathers played at when they were children. The players all seat themselves, like so many tailors, on the floor in a ring, so that their toes all meet. A slipper (the smaller the better) is then produced, and given by the person outside to one sitting in the circle, with instructions that it must be mended by a certain day. Finding it not finished at the time appointed, the pretended owner declares that he must have it as it is, and thereupon commences the hunt. How it is carried on is no doubt too well known to need further explanation.

Parlour games which speak for themselves. The parlour was the room kept for 'best', and normally used by the family on high days and special occasions.

For those with time to spare the range of leisure activities – indoor games, cards, music, sewing, painting, art and reading – has changed little, though each in its way responded to scientific and technological advances made during the 19th century.

Reading

Of all the activities pursued in the home, reading was the most popular. Witnesses attested to a voracious literary appetite in both Great Britain and America by the beginning of the 19th century, and by the end of the century a vast range and variety of books, magazines and newspapers confirmed a growing trend.

The romantic notion of the poor man being read to by his better-qualified neighbour consorts ill with the evidence. Mr Lackington, a London bookseller travelling in America in 1791, was impressed by the fact that reading was a universal pastime.

Surveys conducted in Great Britain by the Society for the Diffusion of Useful Knowledge and the Central Society for Education in the early half of the 19th century found that many working-class homes possessed the Bible and other improving works – such as John Bunyan's *Pilgrim's Progress*. The thirst for knowledge and literary matter was in place before full-time schooling notionally provided the tools and it was rather the cost and availability of reading matter, and the limitations of lighting, that promoted the one reading to the many.

Periodicals and books

With paper available by the reel, the rotary printing press, and automatic typesetting in place, popular magazines began to appear, encouraging literacy, and thus boosting themselves. Much fiction appeared in periodicals and magazines. A glance at a few shows them to be packed with stirring stories of victims, cads and sterling young rescuers. On the other hand Dickens' *Household Words* (1850) and subsequently *All the Year Round* (1859) were two of the earliest popular magazines in Great Britain designed to combine high quality writing with low price. Later, leisure titles such as *Titbits, Answers, Pearson's Weekly* and *The Strand Magazine* (in which Sherlock Holmes made his debut in 1891) all appeared, closely followed by the first halfpenny daily newspaper – the *Daily Mail* – in 1896.

In America, Frank Leslie's *Illustrated Newspaper* appeared in 1855 and *Harper's Weekly* in 1857. Between 1865 and 1888 the number of periodicals jumped from 200 to a phenomenal 3,300 – significantly more than in Britain. The range of topics – in Britain at least – is revealing. Religious journals, having occupied a good 75 per cent in 1860, lost ground through the rest of the century to learned, scientific, female, hobbies and sporting interests, not counting the abundance of trade and general-interest journals.

Books became cheaper and more readily available. Fiction was the most popular. In America before the Civil War *Uncle Tom's Cabin* (1857) was the best-selling work. By the end of the century 'penny dreadfuls' and 'dime shockers' – fictional adventures, romances, spicy melodramas, and thrillers written to a formula – were avidly sought on both sides of the Atlantic. 'Pulp' fiction was introduced in the 1890s – so called because it was printed on poor quality wood-pulp paper. Not that it was all fiction of poor quality. The vast majority certainly was but many classics of the 19th century novel were published in cheap complete versions rather like the Thrift editions today.

'The Americans are addicted to reading newspapers' said Alexis de Tocqueville after his ten-month tour of America in 1830–31. At that time American newspapers carried special features and introduced drawings and cartoons making them more akin to periodicals, but simple newspapers represented another

Cover of *The Wizard of Oz* (1900).

The Wizard of Oz

by L. FRANK BAUM

PICTURES by W.W. DENSLOW

INDOOR GAMES

boom industry during the 19th century.

In 1846, according to *Mitchell's Newspaper Directory,* the 'entire number of dailies in the UK was 14'. By 1860 London alone had 21. Even tiny places such as Devizes, Wells and Wisbech had two each. By 1910 there were 2,331 newspapers in the UK – probably the high water mark. Since then, many have amalgamated or simply gone out of business, but newspaper reading remains the prime source of literary activity on both sides of the Atlantic.

Children's reading matter followed a course not too dissimilar from that of their parents. From stories with an instructive and moralizing element such as *Little Women, Little Lord Fauntleroy, What Katy did*, and *A flat-iron for a farthing* – and even fairy stories were modified

to promote suitable messages – the move into pure entertainment had to wait until after the First World War.

Board games

The first English board games began to appear in the 18th century and were produced in considerable quantities. They were printed on paper, like maps, from engraved copper or steel plates and hand coloured using water-colour. Different copies of the same game could therefore have variations in colour schemes; this was obviated shortly before 1840, when lithographic printing began to replace engraving and hand colouring.

The prepared print was mounted on canvas or linen,

Left Cover of a book of indoor games published about 1905. Compendiums of indoor games date back to 1742.

Wallis's New Game of Universal History and Chronology, first published in London in 1814. The rule book describes the 'Chronology of the most remarkable Events from the Creation to the Present Time.' In this obviously educative and uplifting game for up to 12 players, the first to arrive in the middle comes face to face with His Royal Highness George, Prince of Wales, Regent of the British Empire, is appointed First Lord of the Treasury, and wins all the money.

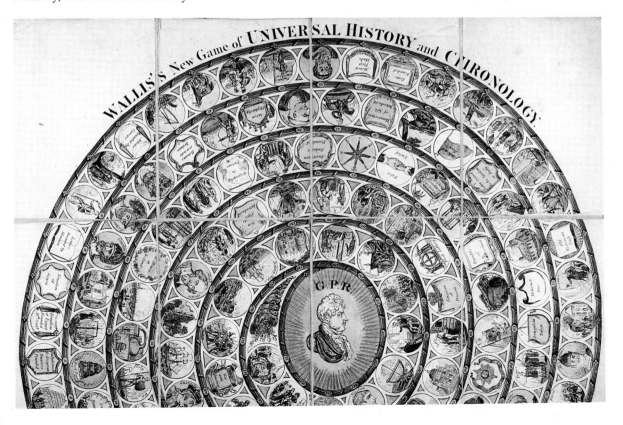

A board game such as 'four in a row' which must have been played with pebbles and boards since the earliest times.

Ayres registered a circular game of *Snakes and Ladders* in 1893. The following year a journalist, R H Harte, patented (No 5586 of 1894) a rectangular version with 34 squares and a 'totum' or spinner in the centre to determine the moves of the players. Landing on a square at the foot of a ladder enables you to ascend; landing on the tail of an arrow sends you to its point. Harte no doubt substituted arrows for snakes as a way round the registered design. In a few years, the board acquired 100 squares, and the snakes – capable of more variety and of causing more frissons than arrows – were reinstated.

folded, and presented in a slip case of thin card. Many London games publishers not surprisingly doubled as map and print sellers, but a sizeable trade in games reflected a considerable public appetite for them.

The French had always been keen board-game players and took up *The Game of the Goose*, a seminal race game, with particular enthusiasm in the 16th and 17th centuries. This game proceeds in a spiral, and appears to have an affinity with Egyptian snake games. Britain's earliest dated game is A Journey through Europe, published in 1759.

Later subjects for board games were nothing if not

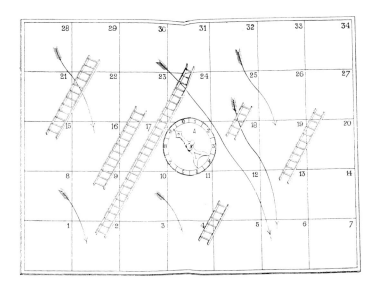

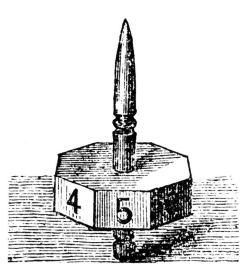

The teetotum is an hexagonal or octagonal top with numbered faces, spun to determine the moves of a game. The teetotum lacked the questionable image of the die, though its users may have been unaware of its associations with the game of 'put and take' which some thought immoral. Put and take uses a four-sided teetotum, with the sides marked N (nothing), P (put into the pool), H (take half the pool), and T (take all the pool). The players sit round with their coins or tokens, putting and taking. Probability ensures that nothing very dramatic happens.

A game of cards – an addition to a manuscript written for Louis II, titular King of Naples, between the years 1352 and 1362.

De la Rue's 1832 patent (6231) for producing playing cards.

topical: *Jeu de la Révolution Française* (1791), *The Comic Game of the Great Exhibition of 1851, Race to the Gold Diggings of Australia* (1852). James Asser introduced *Ludo*, a modification of the classical Indian game *Parchesi* in 1876, and *Snakes and Ladders* appeared in 1892.

Developments in printing certainly helped to hasten the production of games, and in the United States their sales were vastly increased by mail order. Sales were also boosted by manipulative promotional messages from the likes of Frank de Puy who wrote in his *New Century Home Book* (1900): 'In the best and happiest homes games and pastimes have their place. There can be no doubt that men and women are helped to happier and better lives by home amusements.'

Essentially, board games consist in competing players racing tokens round a course, and the most usual way of deciding the extent of each player's move is to throw a die (plural: dice). Originally knucklebones (the Arabic word for 'knucklebone' is the same as that for 'die'), dice had magical associations and were used in casting lots to divine the future. This accounts for much of the moral castigation they periodically suffered; indeed, from the 18th century many games used a hexagonal top or teetotum to divorce themselves from the sinful associations of dice.

Playing cards

In 1832, Thomas de la Rue patented a method of colour printing playing cards, which made their production easier and cheaper. The origin of playing cards appears to date back to Medieval China. Though Chaucer (d1400) does not mention them, we know that they were present in England because of a prohibition order of 1463 – which seems to have affected neither their spread nor their popularity. Playing cards haven't always been associated with games of chance, though it was that particular element above all which occasionally brought them into disrepute. As a child, Louis XIV absorbed a knowledge of heroes, French history, queens, heroines, and geography through cards. In the 18th century, packs were used in teaching arithmetic and grammar.

By the second half of the 19th century, despite the thinking which gave us *Happy Families*, conventional card games of *Cribbage, Whist, Loo*, and *Carilo* had returned to popularity. By 1890, the totally respectable

Mr Pooter on one evening managed to lose the then princely sum of 4 shillings. Card playing ranked with music making as the most popular form of sociable home entertainment. *Bridge* was introduced from the Middle East in the 1880s, but it was some years before it took over from whist. It had the advantage of interminable post mortems which could generate more heat than the game itself.

Sewing and sewing machines

Sewing, in terms of mending and button replacing, was a must for many women and the ability to pursue this activity by artificial light a godsend. Need of course was in inverse proportion to gentility – the more useless, or simply decorative, the working, the more genteel the worker.

From the middle of the century the sewing machine for home use began to appear. The American Isaac Merritt Singer took over sewing machine technology as it was in 1850 and combined with it a flamboyant commercial instinct. Machines were sold door to door and through mail order firms with payments on an instalment plan – hire purchase.

Sewing machines were operated either by hand or by a treadle. Deliberately ornate hand-operated machines were developed to make them seem less like factory implements and more appealing to the feminine domestic market. A Singer electric machine was available from 1889, complete with wet batteries, though electric machines made little commercial impact until after the Second World War. To complement the domestic sewing machine scene Ebenezer Butterick of Massachusetts founded the Butterick Pattern Company in 1863 to produce paper patterns for home dressmakers.

Table games

Many larger homes boasted a games room, principally to house a billiard table. The origin of billiards is shrouded in mystery; the game came to England from Spain in the 16th century. Since the 18th century it has undergone many modifications and spawned the equally-popular snooker and pool.

Snooker played an unexpected part in leisure development in the 1960s in England, when it was chosen as 'a game in which colour is essential' to promote the BBC's colour television service. The effect on colour television may have been marked, but the public interest in snooker took off beyond any promoter's wildest dreams.

Plenty of space was also needed for *Ping Pong*, a game which first appeared as *Gossima* in 1898. Invented by James Gibb a decade or so earlier, the game took off on both sides of the Atlantic in 1901, having been renamed and properly promoted. Clearly the expertise of players varied – witness the number of devices patented for the retrieval of balls from under chairs and in corners, thus obviating the need to go on hands and knees.

Exercising

Home entertainment became more energetic in the decades around the turn of the century when health and exercise began to be taken seriously. Advertisements appear for exercising machines and gymnastic apparatus, as do magazines and journals devoted to the subject. Eliza's husband proposed to take his 'growing size' in hand and deal with it scientifically. He purchased a copy of Mossop's Tyrolean Exercises with chart. Mr Mossop called into play 'exactly the

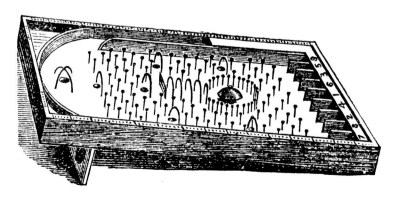

German billiards, otherwise known as Bagatelle. A ball is driven up the chute on the right of the board, often with a spring plunger. It then bounces from pin to pin until it settles in one of the scoring compartments.

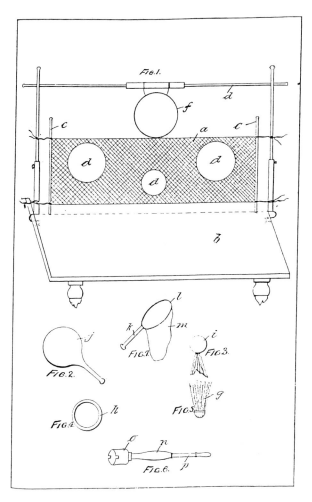

Any success spawns its imitators. Frederick Haynes, a retired master mariner, patented his Improved Table Game in 1902 (No 4982). The net has two or three 'port holes' and a hoop suspended from a rod above. Each of the two players has five shuttlecocks, rings and tailed balls; a bat; a bat bag; and a spring shooter for projecting the shuttlecocks through the holes, whereupon the opponent endeavours to catch them in the bat bag or return them through the holes, doubling the points each time they go through.

same muscles that would be required in, say, an ascent of the Matterhorn, and guaranteed to prevent any undesirable frontal extension.'

Word games and puzzles

The Victorian mind was tickled by riddles and conundrums. Word games such as rebuses, riddles, acrostics, anagrams and so on began to appear during the 18th century. In 1812 Nowell and Burch published *Frolics of the Sphinx*, 'an entirely original collection of charades, riddles and conundrums.' In its chapter 'Fireside Fun', *Cassell's Book of Indoor Amusements* lists 27 such etymological gymnastics. These are accompanied by 23 'Mechanical' puzzles, and, as befits a scientific century, 20 arithmetical puzzles. It says much for them that many of these puzzles still crop up in today's newspapers and periodicals as 'brain teasers'.

Parlour games are not much played today and, along with charades, theatricals, and' tableaux vivants' have – faced with the unequal competition of television – waned in popularity.

Spiritualism

Fashionable in the last quarter of the 19th century was a rising interest in clairvoyance, spiritualism and astrology. *Arcana* and *The Astrologer* were two journals devoted to the subject.

Dabbling with ouija boards (*oui–ja*; French and German for 'yes') and visits from entertaining mediums were accepted social occasions. On ouija boards, Sears Roebuck opined that they were 'without a doubt, the most remarkable and interesting and mystifying production of the age and cannot be sent by mail'.

There was something comforting, perhaps, in being able to communicate with the spirit world, though it is infuriating that the spirits have never seemed able to say anything of lasting interest, let alone hold a coherent conversation from which we might learn something of their being, and hence what to expect.

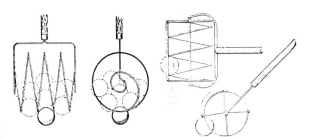

One of many devices for retrieving and raising errant ping pong balls.

DOUBLE END BAGS.

Here is a line of double end bags which are lively, good and can be put up anywhere where you can put in two screw eyes. Illustration shows a bag put up in a doorway. Bore a 1-inch hole in your door sill, turn a screw eye into it so it will be below the sill and out of the way; fasten a hook to the elastic cord and hook it to the screw eye, and you can take down the bag or put it up in a few seconds any time. These prices include the bag, bladder, a piece of rope, two screw eyes, and a piece of elastic cord.

No. 6R6845 Made of gold tan with strong loop. Double end, good, desirable and strong, 30-inch circumference when inflated. Weight, complete, about 14 ounces.

Sears, Roebuck's 'Double End Bag ... lively, good, and can be put up anywhere where you can put in two screw eyes.' The room beyond is shown in mute testimony to the acceptability of these punch bags, which sold for $1.35 up.

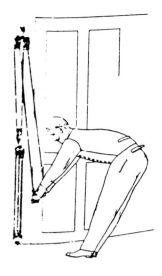

Kühne, Sieves and Neumann's improved patent gymnastic apparatus (No 25,996 of 1901). 'Hitherto, it has been necessary, when a greater strength of apparatus is required, to purchase a complete set of fittings, the others of lesser power thereby being rendered completely useless. This invention makes it possible to regulate the strength of the apparatus so that persons of varying degrees of strength and skill can use it. This is achieved by an arrangement of springs and pulleys, the number of elastic cords attached thereto being variable as desired.'

The Divided Farm – a complicated puzzle.

A Frenchman died leaving five sons, among whom he had expressed a wish to divide his farm, on which ten trees grew, so that they might live together in the house (represented by the dark square in the diagrams), and so that each might have an equal share of the land, of a similar shape, each share having two trees growing upon it. The figure shows the land before it was divided. Turn to page 51 to see how the old man's wishes were carried out.

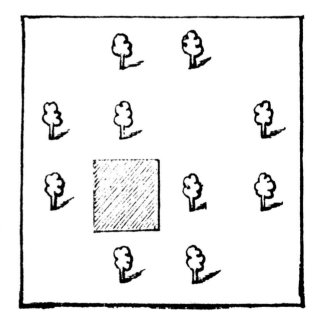

Fashionable curiosities

Many fashionably diverting by-products of the scientific trends of the 18th and 19th centuries became individually available for those with the inclination and the means.

Many of them – optical 'gadgets' for example – must have had limited staying appeal even in those less sophisticated times. Yet technical imaginations must have been fired in those households where enquiry was encouraged and scopes and tropes fell easily off the tongue. Looking back, we can see how the peep shows, the zoetropes, the magic lanterns and the talking machines have matured into the plethora of technology which invades the modern home.

Shadow play, the forerunner of all optical developments, has long and universally been a fascination to the extent that in medieval times the Western church stepped in to control a phenomenon which, in the hands of scientists – or rather magicians – could become dangerous. By the early 19th century, however, things were more relaxed and books of the time give detailed instructions for making screens, cut outs and suitable sources of light.

The diorama and peepshow

An interest in optics had by the 18th century produced telescopes, microscopes and magic lanterns.

A panorama was created by painting long images on cloth, and winding them from one roller to another across an opening frequently resembling a proscenium arch. The audience would be treated to full sound effects from an accompanying band while viewing the scene.

Small versions of these panoramas, known as peepshows, were for individual entertainment. The subjects differed little. Well known are Queen Victoria's Coronation (1838), the Duke of Wellington's Funeral Procession (1852) and scenes from the American Civil War (1861–5). River trips were also popular subjects, as were battles, mutiny on the *Bounty,* and the Great Exhibition held in London in 1851.

The diorama was invented by Louis Daguerre, of photography fame. Dioramas were semi-transparent paintings viewed with a mixture of reflected and transmitted light controlled by windows and mirrors. The scene could thus be viewed as if it were, for example, in bright sunlight or raining. First shown in London in 1823, dioramas also had their drawing-room-scale equivalent, in the candle-lit peepshow, as sold by Ackerman, Spooner and Reeves, a firm of London printers.

The stereoscope

Stereoscopic pictures afforded another way of introducing a feeling of depth into an image. A stereoscopic pair provided two views of the same image, one as seen through the left eye and the other as seen through the right eye. The images were then viewed through two converging lenses so that the images merged into one. The stereoscope was invented by Sir David Brewster in 1816, but awaited the development of photography to realise its full popularity.

The magic lantern

A 1719 dictionary described the magic lantern as 'a little optical machine which enables one to see in the dark on a white wall, many spectres and frightful monsters'. The name of the 13th century writer Roger Bacon had been associated with the magic lantern, and he did not escape the accusation of dabbling in magic. Pope Innocent IV, arbiter in these matters, was fortunately delighted with the effect, so magic lanterns weren't banned out of hand. It is revealing that, until the 18th century, the subject matter tended to have supernatural or religious connotations and messages, featuring ghosts, demons and skeletons.

By the 19th century, according to an optical toy-maker speaking to Henry Mayhew in 1850, when Mayhew was conducting his mammoth survey into the conditions of London's labouring poor: 'Landscapes, Fingal's Cave, cathedrals are most popular now. In the landscapes, we give the changes from

Hand-shadows. 'The illustrations will assist those who wish to amuse children by making rabbits, etc, on the wall. The shadows will be seen perfectly thrown if the hands be carefully fixed near a good light.'

A pair of stereoscopic pictures showing one of the rooms in the Louvre, Paris, about 1870.

Magic lantern amusements for the holiday.

MECHANICAL LANTERN SLIDES.

Lightning Lantern Slide Carrier.
Mahogany, **11**d. Mahogany, with Raising Lever, **1/2** each.
Postage 2d.

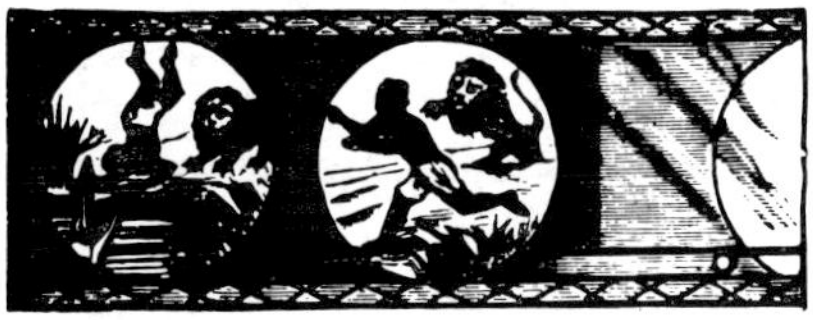

Slipping Slides. With metal frames, for Magic Lanterns, per box of 1 doz. Comic subjects.

1¼ & 1⅝	1⅞	2	2⅛	2½ in.	
2/6	**3/-**	**4/-**	**5/6**	**7/-**	Post 4d. doz

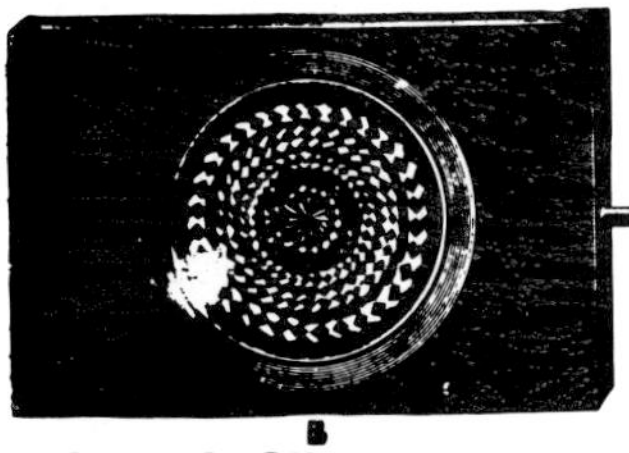

Rackwork Slides. Chromotrope, double rack frame, producing a remarkable combination of coloured effects, by revolving process, hand-painted photographic, **8/-** each. Post 3d. each.

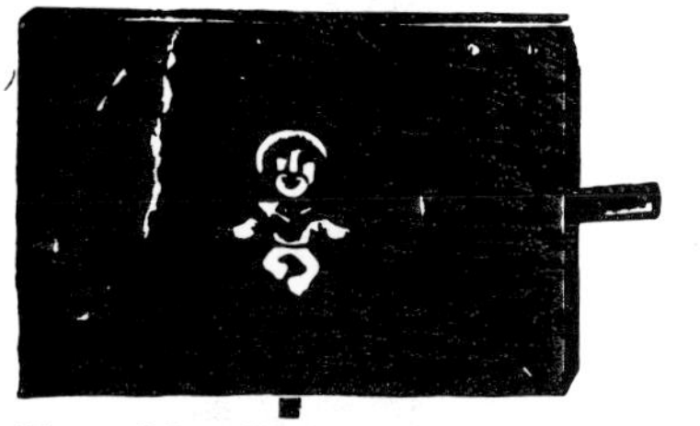

Movable Skipping Slides.
Hand-painted, **3/-** Post 3d. each.

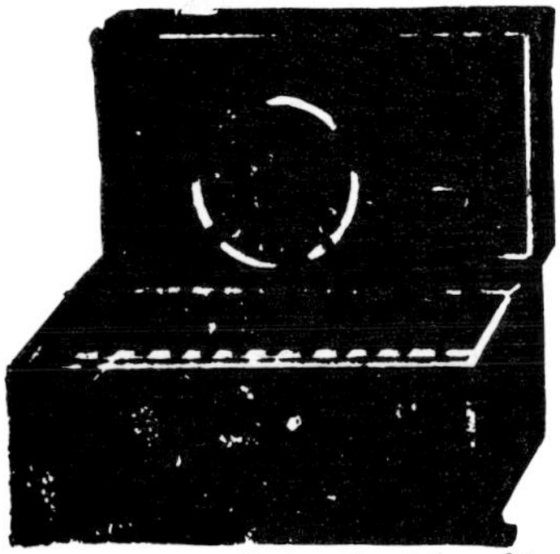

Chromotrope Set. Consisting of 6 pairs coloured discs, producing a variety of different effects; also Rackwork Carrier Frame. The discs can easily be removed at will. Price, complete in wood box for full-sized lanterns, **17/6** Post 9d.

We have an exceptionally large and varied selection of Lantern Slides, Topical Up-to-date Subjects, Humorous, Pathetic, Scientific, &c., to suit every class of audience.

For 'XMAS ENTERTAINMENTS the Magic Lantern is unrivalled, and we have all the popular Slides illustrating Fairy Tales with readings, Comic Tales with readings, and technical slides.

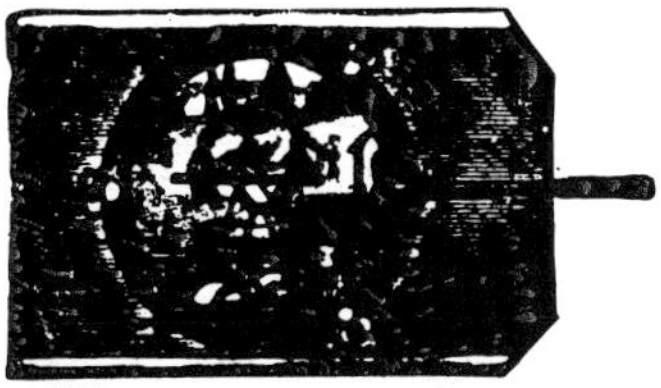

Fig. 5. **Movable Lever Slides.**
In Wood Frames. Comic Subjects.

1⅞	2	2¼	3⅛	3¼ in. wide.
7d.	**9**d.	**1/-**	**1/2**	**1/4** each. Post 4d. doz.

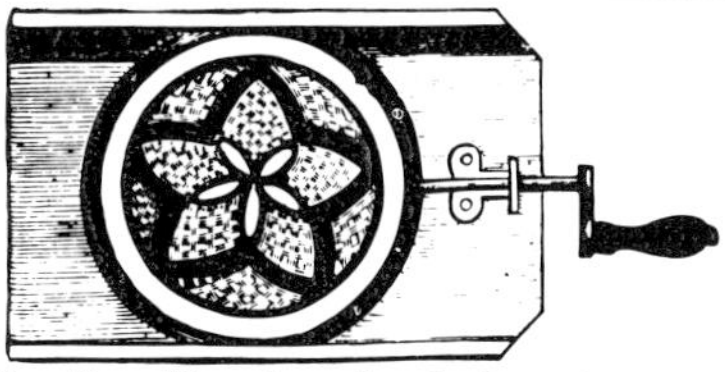

Fig 7. **Mechanical Lantern Slides,** Chromotrope. Post 3d. each.
2 in., **10½**d. 2¾ in., **1/1** 4 in., **1/9** each.
A variety of other effects.

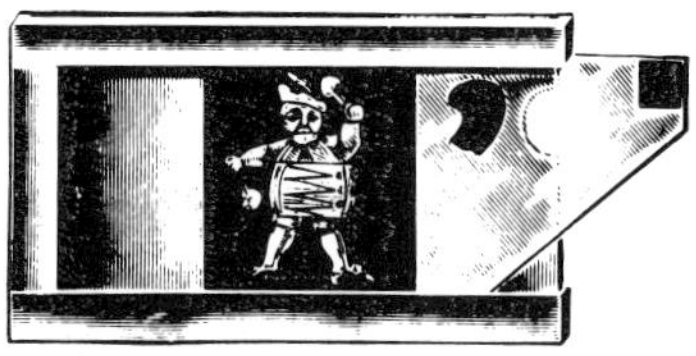

Changing Comic Slipping Slides.
With mahogany frames. Suitable for full-size Lanterns, **6/-** doz. Post 1/- doz.

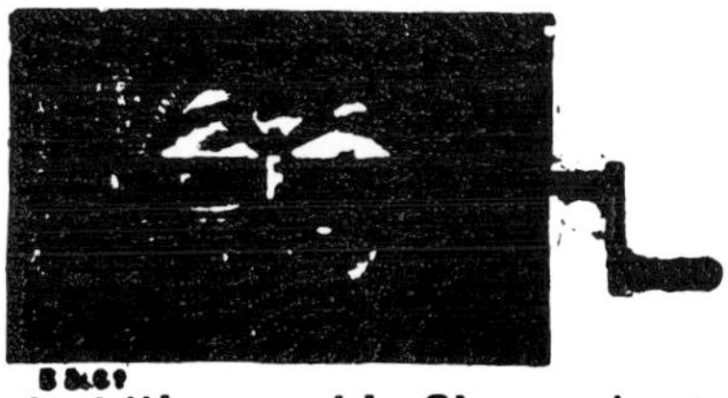

Fig. 8. **Lithographic Chromotrope Rackwork Slides.**
For full-sized Lanterns, **1/9** each. Post 4d. each.

Double Rackwork Chromotropes
Assorted designs. Coloured Lithographic.
2/ each. Post 1/- doz.

Lantern Slide Carriers.
Carrier, giving dissolving effect, as illustration .. **9 10** Postage 4d.

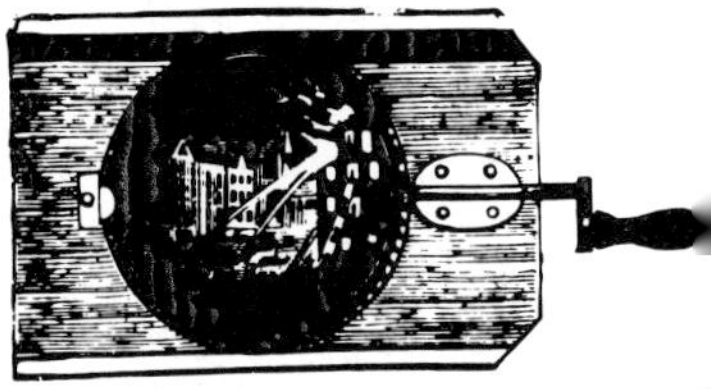

Fig. 9. **Mechanical Rackwork Lantern Slides.** (Fire Scene).

2	2¼	2¾	3¼	3½ in.	
1/4	**1/6**	**1/9**	**1/11**	**2/2** ea.	Post 2d.

A variety of other effects.

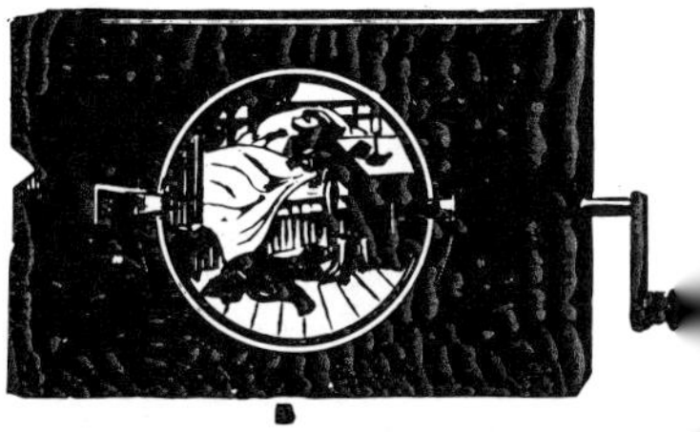

Rackwork Slides (best quality). H[illegible] painted, photographic, double movement. "[illegible] Swallowing Rats," etc., **8/-** each. Post 3d. e[illegible]

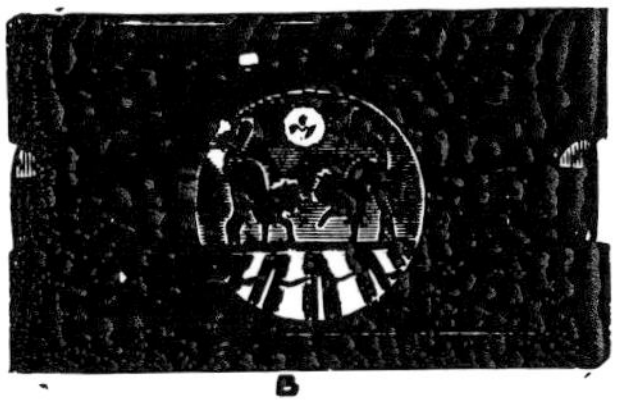

Movable Slides.
Hand-painted Comic subjects. Very amus[illegible]
1/4 each. Post 3d. each.

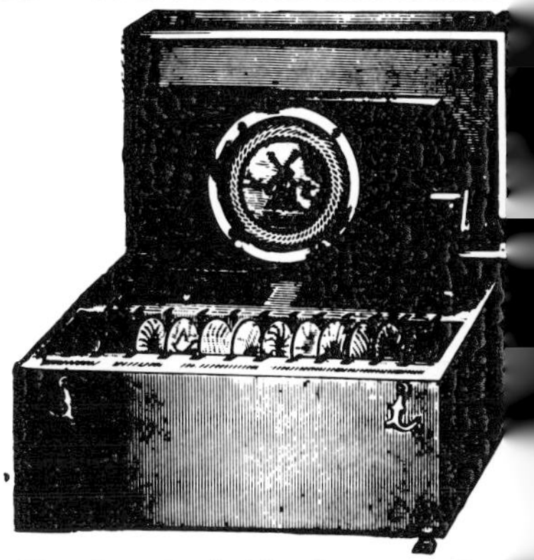

Mechanical Rackwork Se[illegible]
Consisting of 6 hand-painted Lantern Slide [illegible] size), 6 pairs of Coloured discs, and Rac[illegible] Carrier Frame. The slides are inserted at th[illegible] of carrier, and 2 of the discs, 1 on either sid[illegible] used in conjunction with each, which re[illegible] around the fixed slide, producing a beauti[illegible] life-like effect. The discs can easily be re[illegible] at will. Price, complete in wood box, **25**[illegible] [illegible] full-sized Lanterns. Postage 9d.

Dissolving views were achieved by using a double (or even multiple) magic lantern. Moveable masks manipulated by a skilful operator could achieve quite advanced effects.

Right The handle (bottom right) moves the sets of fingers across the lenses, hiding one picture as the other is revealed. The bent chimneys prevented light illuminating the ceiling.

Left The classic Victorian slide is of a sleeping man with a moveable jaw and a series of rats climbing up his bedspread. The sleeping man could be made to swallow each rat in turn. The adventurous operator would, of course, heighten the effect by using suitably exaggerated snoring and lip-smacking effects.

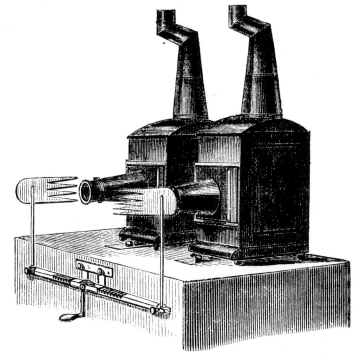

summer to winter – from a bright sun in July to the snow seen actually falling in January.'

The images were painted on glass. Later in the 19th century, separate slips of glass bore different pictures and the skilful operator could, by pulling a lever, make the image appear to move. Clearly, the challenge was to create a plausible moving image. About 1860 a Mr Beale invented a mechanism for rapidly changing the magic lantern slides which he called the 'choreuto-scope'. Apparently the mechanism was fundamentally the same as in future projectors, though at the time not enough was made of the choreutoscope's potential – perhaps, as with many of these ambitious developments, its very name was against it.

Tropes and scopes

A different ingredient was needed before movement became more 'real'. This ingredient came from another family of tropes and scopes which had developed as a result of scientific investigations into the physiological phenomenon known as 'persistence of vision'. The Frenchman P M Roget – probably better known for his Thesaurus – discovered that the retina of the eye could retain an image for about one tenth of a second.

This was intriguingly demonstrated by the thauma-trope invented by Dr J A Paris in 1827. It consisted in a small circular piece of card having a different but associated drawing on each side. When spun rapidly by cords the two images appear to merge – so, for example, the dog enters the kennel, or the rider mounts the horse.

The phenakistiscope (or phenokistoscope, fantas-cope, or magic disk) was invented by the Frenchman Joseph Plateau in 1832. A series of images, for example of a bird in different stages of flight, is drawn on the outer edge of a disk. A simple method of viewing is to cut radial slots between the images; mount the disk with the images away from you, and look through the slots into a mirror as you spin the disk on its centre. When the disk is spun rapidly, the subject appears to move.

The idea of using viewing slits was employed in the zoetrope, or wheel of life, invented in England by William Horner in 1834 and rediscovered and patented by Milton Bradley and Co in the US in 1867. The images are drawn on a strip of paper which is placed circumferentially in a revolvable drum with vertical slits

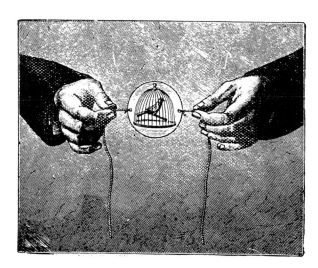

A thaumatrope; the disk has the image of a cage on one side and the bird on the other. When spun by means of twisted cords, the images merge.

Plateau's phenakistiscope, showing a figure skipping. Spin the disks and watch the action through the passing slots.

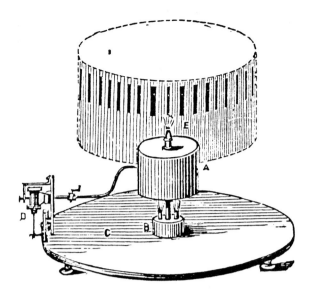

strategically cut. When you turn the drum and look through the passing slits, you will see a continuous action of acrobats, dancers, or whatever is inscribed on the paper strip.

The shortcoming of the zoetrope lay in the slits – the images were not clearly defined, and rather dark. Emile Reynaud's praxinoscope (1877) addressed this problem by using mirrors to reflect the images. The faceted mirror drum was placed inside the drawing drum and was about half the diameter. The images now appeared closer together, and the arrangement enhanced their brightness. Moreover, the moving image could be superimposed upon a background of the viewer's choice.

Two strands of invention – the magic lantern and the zoetrope – now developed and converged in the investigation of machines to take and project series of photographs.

Photography

During the 18th and 19th centuries artists often used the *camera obscura* to help them draw more accurately. It was early noticed that in a darkened room a chink or hole in the blind would project an inverted image of

The zoetrope. The sequence of pictures on a strip is placed round the inside of the drum so that it can be viewed through the slits when the drum is turned. The steam-driven model in the sketch is said to turn at 50 revolutions per minute for 20 minutes.

Below **Six zoetrope strips.**

The praxinoscope theatre. 'The illusion produced by this scientific plaything is very complete and curious, and M Reynaud cannot be too much commended for so cleverly applying his knowledge of physics in the construction of an apparatus which is at the same time both an optical instrument and a charming source of amusement.' It seems as if the operator is so enthralled with the set-up that the girl doesn't get a look in.

the outside scene on the opposite wall. Mirrors and lenses could right the image and improve the clarity. These principles were incorporated into the portable *camera obscura* (dark room) which appeared in the 18th century.

Another optical aid to drawing was the *camera lucida*, wherein a prism was set to reflect a scene on to a sheet of paper. It was the challenge of the desire to 'fix' images of the *camera obscura* by chemical means which led to photography, by means of what became simply a 'camera'.

The first photograph (not surprisingly of an outdoor scene) was taken by the Frenchman Nicéphore Niepce in 1826. It needed an eight-hour exposure. Niepce had started his experiments in 1814, and continued to experiment until his death in 1833. In England, William Henry Fox Talbot took a photograph of a window of his home, Lacock Abbey, in 1835; exposure time 30 minutes. Fox Talbot's great contribution was the negative–positive process, which he announced in 1839. Later that year, Louis Daguerre, proprietor of the Paris

Reversed image of a landscape projected by a hole in a blind.

The portable *camera obscura* in which a mirror and lens on the rotating turret focus an image on to the artist's pad.

Diorama (who had been in partnership with Niepce) perfected his 'Daguerrotype' process, and the new hobby of photography was established.

Cameras and photographic supplies were on sale from 1839, and photography was soon established both as a means of recording events and making portraits, and as a hobby. At first, photographers would prepare and develop their own 'plates'; later plates could be bought and developing services were available. The step forward was in 1881 when Alfred Pumphrey of Birmingham patented a camera 'film' (as opposed to a plate). John Carbutt of Philadelphia announced film on celluloid in 1888, and George Eastman (1859–1932) of Rochester, NY introduced roll film for his Kodak camera that same year.

Eastman's ambition was to make photography as simple as possible so that anyone could take 'snaps', and the roll film enabled him to do this. A friend told Eastman that the public was attracted to names containing the letter 'k'; 'Kodak' should therefore be twice as attractive. Whether or not it was the reason, the word 'Kodak' became synonymous with simple, effective photography for all.

In spite of all modern developments and automation, the anatomy of the camera has not changed in 100 years. The first Kodak was a box 16.5 x 9 x 9 cm (6.5 x 3.5 x 3.5 in), and contained a 100-exposure roll film. It had a fixed focus lens, one speed and one stop. All you had to do was to point it at the scene, click the shutter, and all the scene beyond 2.4m (8ft) would be captured in focus. You could then send the camera to Kodak who would develop the film, mount the prints, and send it back reloaded. The slogan was: 'You press the button, we do the rest'; thus did Eastman do more than anyone else to popularize photography.

Cinematography

It's always a mistake to assume the end product or the gadget we know today was the one originally foreseen by its early inventors and developers. The ability to show sequential images led to an increased scientific interest in the movements of animals. This in turn led to a concentration of effort into the investigation of photographic exposure times, as such minute changes of movement could not easily be drawn; witness Eadweard Muybridge's experiments in California in 1879 photographing galloping horses, and Professor Marey's work in France with the movements of birds' wings.

In 1882, Eadweard Muybridge (an Englishman who, having been acquitted of murdering his wife, changed his name from Edward Muggeridge and emigrated to America) showed his galloping horse photographs by means of his zoopraxiscope, a projecting phenokistoscope which incorporated the new electric arc lamp.

George Eastman had pioneered the use of flexible celluloid instead of heavy glass plates to carry the

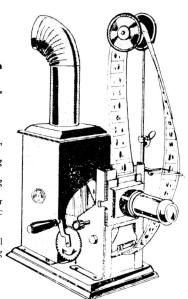

Miniature Combination Cinematograph and Magic Lantern.

No. 786. Strongly made, iron body, mounted on metal base, fitted with lens, condenser, and paraffin lamp. 3 long coloured films are supplied for producing the living pictures. Provision is made for using ordinary magic lantern slides, 1¾ in. wide. Price, complete in box with full instructions, including 6 slides, **12/6**

Postage 9d.

Post free.

An unsophisticated short-film projector, price 12/6d. The numerous films included *An Indian ballet*, *The King leaving Buckingham Palace* and *A Canadian express train*.

Right Edison's 1901 kinetoscope, price $105. Films included *The assassination of President McKinley*, and *The life and daily happenings of a fireman*.

DEPARTMENT OF MOVING PICTURE OUTFITS.

THIS IS UNDOUBTEDLY THE MOST NOVEL, THE MOST INTERESTING AND THE MOST POPULAR FORM OF PUBLIC ENTERTAINMENT WHICH IS NOW BEING PRESENTED AND ONE WHICH OFFERS A WIDER FIELD AND GREATER RETURNS FOR THE MONEY INVESTED THAN ANY OTHER SPECIES OF PUBLIC ENTERTAINMENT.

THE MOVING PICTURE APPARATUS, although used in combination with the stereopticon, must not be confounded with it. The Magic Lantern or Stereopticon shows merely the stationary pictures with which all have been familiar for years, the moving picture machine, however, is of comparatively recent invention, and projects moving pictures lifelike and of life size upon a screen or canvas. It undoubtedly represents the highest branch in the art of photography and illuminated picture projections and brings before the eye an exact and life size reproduction, with all the accompanying effects of light, shadow and expression. We have always been in the forefront of dealers in handling this type of outfit. We have made a study of this branch of the exhibition business. For the past three years the manager of this department has come in personal contact with more exhibitors, has corresponded with a larger number of successful operators than probably any man in the United States. We know what is needed to build up a successful exhibition. We place our knowledge and our experience at the disposal of any purchaser or prospective purchaser absolutely free of charge. We advise him to the best of our ability whether he does or does not purchase an outfit, and we are able to assist him in his final selection by pointing out to him outfits which will make his success certain, and subjects for his exhibition which will insure him an audience wherever he advertises, and guarantee him in successfully entertaining them.

WE GUARANTEE EVERY MACHINE, every outfit which we send out. We have an established reputation in this line to support. Those who have dealt with us do not require any assurance of this, but to those who have not, we say, that any outfit sent out by us can be thoroughly tested, tried and examined at the customer's house and if not exactly as represented, up to standard and capable of the most effective work, we not only permit but we ask that you return it to us within a reasonable time from its receipt and we will refund whatever money you have paid for it.

THE EDISON 1901 KINETOSCOPE.
(IMPROVED MODEL)

THIS SEASON we shall handle the Edison Kinetoscope for projecting moving pictures exclusively. The moving picture apparatus is known as one of the greatest of the Edison inventions, and on the Wizard of Originality has spent much time in the perfection of the present type of machine, embodying every improvement and every convenience which science, mechanical skill and research have been able to add to the first invention. The machine is handsome, durable and complete in every detail.

PORTABILITY. Weighs, when fully equipped, only 55 pounds, and can be packed in one case or be packed in an ordinary trunk and shipped as baggage.

SIMPLICITY. The machine is easily set up and operated; every instrument is accompanied by full directions. An amateur can operate it as well as a professional.

SCIENTIFIC ACCURACY. Every detail has been so carefully planned that the result is a steady and brilliant picture, and any scratching or injury to films is reduced to a minimum.

SIZE OF PICTURE. The size of the picture which can be projected with this machine is unlimited; it depends only upon the distance at which it is set from the screen. Twelve hundred feet of film can be used on this machine at one time in one continuous roll.

SUPERIORITY OF CONSTRUCTION. The machine is constructed at the Edison factory, under the immediate supervision of the inventor, a statement which assures as near an approach to perfection as is mechanically possible. It includes many devices and many improvements which until the present year were entirely unknown.

THE FRAMING DEVICE, which is new to this machine, is simple and strikingly effective. By merely adjusting a lever the entire mechanism which holds the film is moved up and down, enabling the operator to frame his film in the fraction of a second.

NO RISK OF HARASSING LITIGATION. The United States court has handed down a decision holding that the Edison Manufacturing Company is entitled to claim priority patent on moving picture machines and films. THE EDISON 1901 KINETOSCOPE is the best. It is the perfected model which gives the best results, and is the only machine with which the exhibitor can, in view of recent legal decision, be free from harassing litigation.

MOVING OR ANIMATED PICTURES are just as popular and even more so than ever before. They possess a merit which increases their popularity every time they are shown, and they are, by this time, so well advertised that the mere announcement of a moving picture entertainment is sufficient to bring out every entertainment lover or frequenter of this class of exhibitions.

THE MOVING PICTURE OUTFIT may be shortly described as made up of three principal items outside of the small and less considered accessories; these are, first: The moving picture machine or apparatus itself, upon which the most depends and in the choice of which the frankest and most careful advice is offered to our patrons, and an absolute guarantee given with the machine. Without a high grade projecting instrument, such as we furnish, the most talented operator can do nothing, and the small amount saved by purchasing an inferior or lower grade machine is money worse than wasted; it is not only thrown away, so far as the moving picture outfit is concerned, but tends to bring the entire exhibition into disrepute owing to its inferiority. Irrespective of price entirely, we have always endeavored to present, for our customers' consideration, the best instrument procurable, and we are pleased to announce that in the Edison Improved Kinetoscope, 1901 model, combined with stereopticon, we are able to furnish our customers with the highest grade of instrument for projecting both moving and stationary pictures which ingenuity, time, effort and experiment have ever produced.

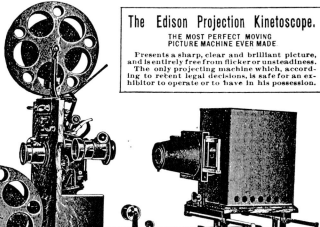

The Edison Projection Kinetoscope.
THE MOST PERFECT MOVING PICTURE MACHINE EVER MADE.

Presents a sharp, clear and brilliant picture, and is entirely free from flicker or unsteadiness. The only projecting machine which, according to recent legal decisions, is safe for an exhibitor to operate or to have in his possession.

No. 21R400 1901 Edison Projecting Kinetoscope and Combined Stereopticon, furnished with electric arc lamp and rheostat for reducing current. Price...$105.00
No. 21R401 1901 Model Kinetoscope and Combined Stereopticon, with latest type of calcium burner and rubber adjustment to make connections for calcium light. Price... 105.00
No. 21R402 Kinetoscope Front for adding the Edison moving picture feature to any stereopticon or professional magic lantern. Price... 75.00
No. 21R405 Improved Take Up Device, for rewinding film; can be attached to any Edison Kinetoscope, if desired. Price... 10.00

WE ARE EXCLUSIVE DEALERS IN THE EDISON MACHINE AND FILMS.
THREE REASONS which now make it more than ever profitable for the exhibitor to start out with a moving picture machine are: FIRST, The improved machine will add efficiency and improve the outfit to an extent that has hardly yet been realized. SECOND, The slightly increased cost will, in many instances, prevent incompetent persons from entering the field, thus deterring those who could and would successfully handle an exhibition of this kind. THIRD, The mechanical perfection obtained in the construction of this machine is such as to insure its being always in order and no annoying inconvenience from break down or for repairs need be feared.

FILMS FOR PROJECTION OF MOVING PICTURES.

NEXT TO THE INSTRUMENT for projecting moving pictures, the film which contains the pictures themselves is the most important item. The film is a long celluloid tape usually about 50 feet, with a series of photographs taken at the rate of forty every second, in order to produce the animated movement for passing rapidly before the projecting lens at the same rate of speed from the beginning to the end of the film, thus reproducing all the movements which were in view when the picture was taken.

For Each Subject a Separate Film is Necessary.

THE FILMS which we handle are exclusively made in the Edison laboratory, and the results obtained surpass anything which has hitherto been produced. A complete revolution in the printing and development departments, the employment of an entirely new process, and the care exercised in scrutinizing and inspecting every film before it is sent from the factory, has resulted in a clearness of definition and a mellow tone, which although long sought for by leading exhibitors, has never been obtained before.

SEE NEXT PAGE for description of various lights used in Moving Picture Work.

WE CARRY SO LARGE A STOCK of these films on hand to fill orders as promptly as received, that it is well nigh impossible to give a detailed list in this place. We publish, however an elegant booklet containing names and description of the latest films. We supplement this list with monthly statements of all new films as they are taken, and upon receipt of postal card we will send free of cost this list and will place name upon our mailing list, so that our customers may keep posted in regard to the latest subjects. A few of the many subjects at present on hand, which will suffice to indicate the wide range we cover, are as follows:
Set of films descriptive of the sublime representation of the Passion Play as given at Oberammergau, Bavaria, of most intense interest not only to churches and religious bodies, but to all classes of people.
Films descriptive of scenes and incidents in connection with the assassination of our late president, Wm. McKinley. The events which transpired at the Buffalo Fair, the funeral cortege in that city, the lying in state at Washington and the interment at Canton.
The Life and Daily Happenings to a Fireman, faithfully portrayed in the wonderful series of unequaled moving picture films.
Pan-American Exposition at Buffalo is reproduced by another set of films.
Our Railway Series shows trains in motion, limited express trains at full speed, etc.
War Films are immensely popular at the present time. The Boer-British war, the war in the Philippines and the Chinese war are all admirably illustrated by our special sets, made up for the purpose.
Yacht Racing and Ocean Scenes are also thoroughly illustrated, including the recent victory of the Columbia over the Shamrock.
The Funeral of Victoria, the late English Queen.
Camp Incidents, Indian Dances and Customs, and Panoramic Scenes of Niagara Falls, while lighter subjects are represented by comic scenes of the most amusing description, graceful dances, exciting horse races and the latest representation of mystical, magical and sensational films.

photosensitive emulsions, and this led to the development of the cinematograph camera able to take up to 20 pictures per second.

The American mutoscope used prints made from film negatives bound together in a reel so that they could flick past the viewer. The mutoscope appeared in public places with mildly erotic pictures; the drawing-room equivalent was the kinora. Reels could be bought or exchanged at libraries and showed the wealthy and the famous, as well as interesting events. A home camera was available for the enthusiast and the kinora projection system remained popular until home movie cameras were introduced by Kodak and Path in the 1920s. With the development of magnetic tape and video cameras, today's home movie director has not only colour and sound but instant replay at the fingertips.

The phonograph

If capturing and reproducing images were one side of the 19th century entertainment technology, the other – and vastly more popular – side was capturing and reproducing sound.

Musical boxes had reached perfection in the 18th century and continued throughout the 19th century to be the only machine to provide music for listening in the home. Originally pins in a revolving barrel struck the tuned teeth of a comb. By the end of the 19th century it became clear that punched discs were easier to operate and cheaper to manufacture than cylinders – a story to be repeated more famously elsewhere.

The development of a machine to record real sound, as opposed to the mechanical sound of the musical box, was first taken up by Thomas Edison. The story of the early development of machines to record and reproduce talking properly belongs to a discussion of early office machines, as both Edison and his early competitors – Charles Sumner Tainter and Chichester Bell – were looking into dictating machines, not musical entertainment machines. Edison produced his first 'talking machine' in 1877, with the idea that it would be used for dictating letters.

Edison's talking machine was not an instant success, largely because it was so difficult to understand the reproduced voice. In 1886, Tainter and Bell patented the Graphophone in America. This was an improvement on Edison's machine because the vibrations were impressed on the surface of a waxed cardboard cylinder, rather than softer tin foil.

Edison returned to the scene in 1888 with his Perfected Phonograph. The cylinders were entirely of wax, which meant they could be shaved and re-used; they played for about two minutes. Both the Phonograph and Graphophone were worked by a treadle or, less commonly, an electric motor. The sound was reproduced down tubes which were fitted into the ear.

The Gramophone was invented by Emil Berliner and appeared in 1888. It used discs as opposed to cylinders, with the stylus cutting a spiral groove into the wax; the profile of the groove was modulated by the sound, at first up and down; later side to side. The groove was deeper than that on a wax cylinder, so no

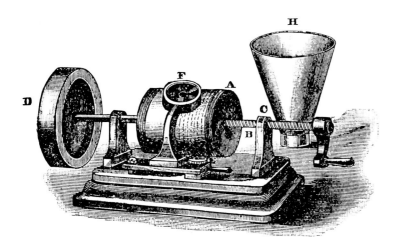

Edison's original phonograph. The cone (H) is attached to diaphragm ring (F). The operator speaks into the cone, and the vibrations of the speech cause a stylus to indent the foil covering of a cylinder (A), working along a guide groove. The cylinder is turned by hand and moved laterally by means of a screw (B) working in support (C). The flywheel (D) helps to keep the movement smooth. The reproducing stylus follows the same groove, and the sound is heard when the diaphragm vibrates.

Edison and the improved phonograph after working three days and three nights on the machine. The photograph was long used to illustrate Edison's dictum: 'Invention is one per cent inspiration and 99 per cent perspiration.'

Right
Berliner's recording machine.

Thomas Broadbent, an engineer, and Reginald Payne, a violin maker, patented an improved instrument for reproducing sound (No 3723 of 1903). It rendered musical sounds or articulate speech more akin to the original 'by combining with the record a box-like resonating chamber such as a violin body, mounted so as to allow a stylus attached to it to follow the grooves in the record. A trumpet is not required.'

Nipper's famous pose. At Berliner's request, the phonograph in the original painting was changed to a Gramophone and the image stayed with the company – as HMV.

feed screw was needed to keep the stylus in the groove. Berliner's machines could therefore be made more cheaply than the Phonograph or Graphophone. Moreover, it is far easier to make pressings of the surface of a disc than of the surface of a cylinder, so 'records' were cheaper, too. The sound was louder than that from a cylinder but hardly clearer. The first discs played for about a minute.

Gramophones were, by and large, driven manually until 1896 when Eldridge R Johnson from New Jersey produced a powerful spring motor. The year after he produced an improved sound box. He started his own company in 1899, calling his gramophones 'Victors'.

Recording artists always preferred recording on to discs as, unlike the cylinders, many pressings could be reproduced from one master.

In 1898, Berliner's company opened a branch in London – The Gramophone Company. The next year the company bought what must rank as the most famous trademark in the entertainments industry: Francis Barraud's painting of his dog Nipper listening intently to a phonograph: 'His Master's Voice'.

Cylinder machines had become popular for home entertainment on both sides of the Atlantic before the

close of the century, despite the fact that there were various manufacturing problems with pre-recorded cylinders. The problem was to find a process for electroplating a wax master for a mould and then finding a suitable thermoplastic wax compound which would shrink cleanly from the mould to make the copies. By the time these problems were overcome discs played longer, and were cheaper and easier to store – and were louder, since the amplifying horn was now common to all playback machines.

In 1903 12-inch discs were produced with a playing time of about four minutes. Attempts were made to increase this; Neophone, for example, produced 20-inch discs of wax on cardboard. These played for between eight and ten minutes but involved producing a vast new machine to accommodate them – for which there was insufficient public support. The standard became the 10-inch disc, though some popular music was produced on 8-inch or even smaller discs. The playing-time barrier was not overcome until the arrival of LPs after the Second World War.

Just before the Depression broke in the United States, electrical recording was introduced and electrical reproduction began to replace the horn. All-electric gramophones (phonographs) appeared in 1925, though they were very expensive. By now radio was beginning to overtake them in popularity, and sales plummeted. However, pick-up kits for wind-up gramophones came on to the market and, connected to the amplifier of the radio, gave a great boost to the quality of reproduction. The next step was the 'radiogram', but few were sold before the Second World War, largely because of the price. Wind-up gramophones were still popular, even after the War.

In America at least, the phonograph replaced most other forms of home music making. In Great Britain the most popular recordings were of operatic stars. This very fact must reflect the sort of people who were interested and rich enough to invest in these new machines. Records by the Russian operatic bass Chaliapin (1873–1938) sold at £1 each on a special red label, while those cut by the Australian operatic soprano Dame Nellie Melba (1861–1931) sold at 1 guinea on a purple one. Classical instrumentalists were encouraged to make recordings. A complete opera was recorded as early as 1903, but this must have had more historic than commercial appeal. Given the short playback

time of each disc, storage of the set alone must have presented some problem. In April 1909, a recording of *The Nutcracker Suite* took three days to make and cost £800.

From advertisers' sheets of the time, we gather that American buying taste was rather different. An act by Russell Hunting in which he played both an Irishman called Casey and a straight man enjoyed enormous success, as did Sousa marches and black artists. Many serious music lovers were unable to come to terms with having their favourite pieces fragmented on to an album full of discs, so recording companies ransacked the repertoire for suitably short works. No wonder the record industry and the popular music industry fed off one another in those days of limited playing time. Discs began to determine the course of popular music as tunes were first adapted and then composed to fit in with the three- or four-minute playing time of records.

The wireless

Even more than the phonograph and gramophone, radio and then television brought standardized entertainment to homes in Great Britain and the United States – standardized in that the listener or viewer had to accept what was being transmitted, or turn off.

At first, both the telephone and wireless telegraphy found more use in commerce and military spheres than in the home. But, as it did with so many other things, the First World War gave wireless telephony a great boost, and as soon as the war was over the Marconi Company at Chelmsford began to set up a series of transmitters of ever greater power.

In the early months of 1920, Marconi transmitted news items, and vocal and instrumental music, on a wavelength of 2,800m for two half-hourly periods each day. Ships (one of the earliest beneficiaries of wireless telegraphy) received the Chelmsford transmissions at distances of over 100 miles (160km), reporting 'good speech' even when using only standard crystal receivers.

In the same year, the *Daily Mail* installed a wireless transmitter at its London offices to transmit special news items to its reporters at Chelmsford. The following month, a special broadcast concert was arranged at which Dame Nellie Melba was heard by 'listeners-in' all over Europe – not to mention in St John's Newfoundland, a distance of 2,673 miles (4,300km).

Now that there were broadcasts to be heard, building 'wireless sets' became a craze. You can still build a very simple receiver using nothing more than a suitable length of wire, a crystal detector, and a pair of headphones. The hobby had the advantage that anyone could do it – and thousands did. As more and more stations around the world began to transmit, the electronic equivalent of twitchers and gricers set up their receiving apparatus and began to collect hearings, paving the way for an industry which, at its lowest level, enables people to talk to one another about the niceties of the equipment they're using to talk to one another.

2MT, the Marconi Scientific Instrument Company station at Writtle, began to transmit on 14 February 1922 with half an hour's transmission of vocal and gramophone selections on a wavelength of 700m and a series of calibration signals on 1,000m.

According to one commentator: 'often a one-man show, Writtle established an individuality all its own which will ever remain a pleasant memory to its broad-

cast audience. Its burlesque entertainments, its parodies of grand opera, its announcements, which were never dull, the light-hearted spirit which pervaded the whole proceedings and which "got across" the æther, were all features admirably suited to the art in its then immature state, which could amuse, but was not yet capable of doing full justice to musical composition.'

The London Broadcasting station at Marconi House (2LO) started to transmit on 14 November 1922, and Writtle ceased a few weeks later. The British Broadcasting Company – later the British Broadcasting Corporation, or BBC – was registered on 15 December 1922 after a great deal of effort to agree a formal licence for its operation with the Postmaster-General. Local stations had opened – and were opening – in cities throughout the kingdom and in April 1923 87,561 broadcasting licences and 32,285 experimental licences had been issued. It was estimated that the number of users of home-made sets without licences was at least 200,000.

As a fitting conclusion to a year's programme of enterprise and successful endeavour, all stations broadcast the striking of Big Ben at midnight on 31 December 1923.

Although home 'listeners-in' tended to use the crystal set (that is, a set with a crystal detector) at first, the English physicist J A Fleming had invented a 'diode' which would perform the same function in 1904. Moreover, the American Lee De Forest had invented the amplifying triode two years later. It was not long before the valve replaced the crystal and amplifying stages were added before and after it to produce two- three- or whatever-valve set. The superior results compensated for the need for wet accumulators (which needed periodical recharging) to drive the valve fila-

Radio in the village. With the coming of wireless, dwellers in the country found much of the life of the great cities brought to their lonely cottages. Each tiny hamlet has its local expert – in this case the village wheelwright – who installed most of the sets in the neighbourhood.

Right **The Air King Three – a three-valve wireless set for the home constructor (1933). The Free Gift Transfer made it 'impossible to make a mistake in the wiring.'**

ALL RADIO
QUESTIONS
ANSWERED
FREE.

The PRACTICAL MECHANICS Wireless Experimenter

Every Question must be accompanied by the Coupon on page 52.

tivity and Simplicity

designing the present receiver it was
cided that, provided ample selectivity for
normal requirements could be secured,
cost and simplicity of construction and
ation should be the main features. Iron
tuning coils were at once ruled out on
grounds of their expense, whilst it was
dered that band-pass tuning should
be employed, due to the fact that it
d necessitate a fair amount of initial
tching," which
proves a stum-
block to the
ge amateur. It
t seem that the
nation of these
modern refine-
s was a retro-
step, but the
s obtained from
finished receiver
otherwise. By
sing suitable air-
coils of high
ency and carefully
ning the circuit
d them it has
found possible to
ve a measure of
ncy even greater
that shown by
receivers of more
licated and expen-
lesign. The wiring
ightfully easy by
s of our Free Gift
fer Print. Illus-
ns showing how
se this are given
20.

Break-through"

has been men-
d that selectivity
ne of the main points considered, but
to this the question of "break-
gh" of the local medium wave station
listening on the long waves was given
I thought. Many otherwise selective
ers suffer from "break-through," and
s often sufficiently severe to prevent
od reception of such long wave trans-
's as Radio Paris, Warsaw and Huizen.
rm of interference is more pronounced
e localities than in others, so in
t to be described provision has
nade for connecting the aerial to
ial tapping on the
il, when required, so
"break-through" can
y be overcome in the
mplest manner.

Output —Easy Tuning

only has the set a
ange, due to the use
efficient variable-mu
d grid amplifier, but
apable of giving the
ely good undistorted
output of 500 milli-
Additionally, how-
there is a useful

THE AIR KING THREE

A new and economical Three-valve Battery Receiver of High Efficiency

By means of our Free Gift Transfer Print it is impossible to make a mistake in the wiring.

volume control acting upon the variable-mu
valve by which the strength of the most
powerful station can, if necessary, be
reduced to a whisper without in any

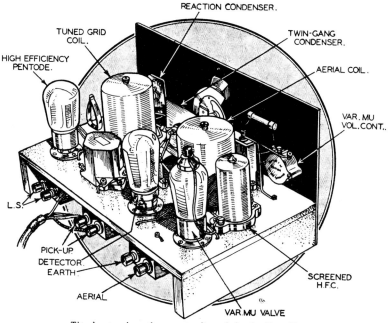

This drawing shows the attractive lines of the Air King Three.

way affecting the quality of reproduction.
Tuning is very easy and is carried out by
operating a dual gang condenser by means
of a single knob. But in order that the very
best may be obtained from the set on weaker
and more distant stations a trimmer is provided, and this is easily adjusted through a
small knob which is concentric with the
main tuning control. There is a reaction
control, and although this is not required
when listening to the more powerful transmitters, it is useful in getting the best from
distant stations and provides a convenient
means of increasing selectivity.

Low Current Consumption

Due to the use of a complete system of
decoupling and volt-
age - regulating resist-
ances, there are only
two high-tension leads
and these may be con-
nected to the battery
specified or to any
eliminator giving an
output of about 12
milliamps. at 120 volts.
When using the 108-
volt H.T. battery the
current consumption is
between 7 and 10 milli-
amps., depending upon
the setting of the
variable-mu volume
control, and therefore
the battery can be
expected to last for
three or four months
before replacement be-
comes necessary. The
low tension current is
only 0·4 amp., and thus
the accumulator will
last for approximately
100 hours on each
charge.

One rather important
refinement of this set is
in the use of an entirely
new metallised wooden
chassis and internally
metallised cabinet. The former has all the
advantages of an aluminium chassis but is
much easier to deal with and somewhat
more rigid. It simplifies the wiring very
considerably, since a number of "earth
return" leads can be attached directly to
it by means of screws. The
cabinet is instrumental in
reducing to a minimum any
direct pick-up from the local
station and also tends to
eliminate interference from
electrical apparatus. It need
not be mentioned that both
the cabinet and the com-
plete receiver are of very
handsome appearance, since
this is evident from the
photographs reproduced on
this and the following pages.

Cheap to Construct

In spite of the many novel
features referred to above,
and though the set is probably as good as any three-
valve battery receiver available, it can be built complete
with loud speaker, batteries,

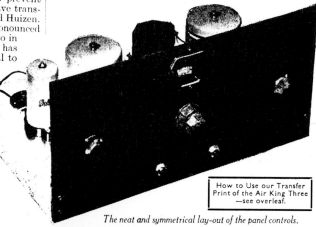

How to Use our Transfer Print of the Air King Three —see overleaf.

The neat and symmetrical lay-out of the panel controls.

ments, and grid bias and HT batteries.

The first known radio programme in the US was broadcast by Reginald Aubrey Fessenden from his experimental station at Brant Rock Massachusetts on Christmas Eve 1906. The programme – of two musical items, a poem and a short talk – was picked up by ships' wireless operators within a radius of several hundred miles.

As a result of the relaxation of military restrictions on radio at the close of the First World War, many experimental stations were set up and operated by amateurs. David Sarnoff, later in charge of the Radio Corporation of America (RCA), had already envisaged in 1916 the possibility of a radio receiver in every home.

RCA was set up in 1919 in order to acquire the American subsidiary of the British company Marconi Wireless; at the time it was the only company capable of handling commercial transatlantic radio and the Americans were anxious to keep their hands on the current technology.

The evolution of commercial broadcasting went rap-idly forward. Entertainment was in demand as were sets suitable for a layman. The demand justified the establishment of stations. The first commercial radio station was KDKA in Pittsburgh, Pennsylvania which went on the air November 1920. Eight stations were operating in the US by the end of the following year, but a staggering 564 were licensed by the end of 1922. As an article in the American Review of Reviews of 1923 put it: '"Listening in" became the new national pleasure.' By 1924 five million American homes owned a radio receiver.

There were two possible sources of financial support; profits from the manufacture and sale of equipment or revenue from commercial advertisers. This latter was the eventual route in America. 'Soap operas' date from the mid-1920s with soap manufacturers sponsoring programmes and story-lines with special appeal to those at home during the day.

The development of radio as purveyor of entertainment and information (both in the US and the UK) contrasted strongly and was keenly felt by many

Portable transmitting and receiving sets 'originally designed for transport on mule back in a tropical country where they would be subjected to very rough usage.' The transmitter works on the original Marconi principle.

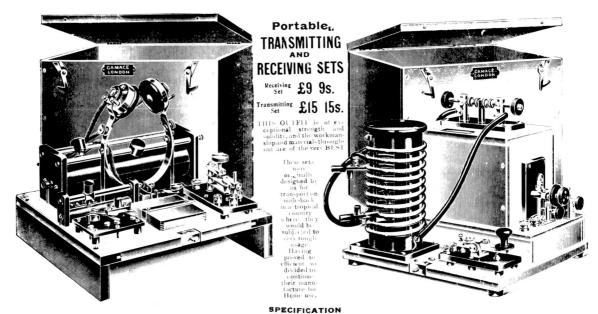

Portable

TRANSMITTING

AND

RECEIVING SETS

Receiving Set **£9 9s.**

Transmitting Set **£15 15s.**

THIS OUTFIT is of exceptional strength and solidity, and the workmanship and materials throughout are of the very BEST

These sets were originally designed by us for transport on mule-back in a tropical country where they would be subjected to very rough usage. Having proved so efficient we decided to continue their manufacture for Home use.

SPECIFICATION

Receiving—Two-slide inductance with ebonite mountings
Crystal Detectors mounted on ebonite with four combinations.
Potentiometer with ebonite slider, knob and ends
Ebonite Switch for cutting out Potentiometer and Local Battery
Change-over Switch for Sending to Receiving
Blocking Condenser and 2,000 Ohms Double Headgear

Sending—High-speed Wireless Coil with Patent Interruptor
Series Spark Gap mounted on ebonite
Oscillation Transformer of Copper Tube, mounted on ebonite
Sending Key mounted on ebonite
Bases and Cabinets of teak

Americans. In 1947 the radio pioneer Lee De Forest lamented that what could have been a 'potent instrumentality for culture, fine music and the uplifting of America's mass intelligence' had instead become 'a laughing stock that resolutely kept the average intelligence at 13 years.'

Television

Hand in hand with the development of radio walked the child television. However, the equipment needed for television was much less simple than that for radio, and its applications were less obviously practical.

Television, like other optical developments, depends upon persistence of vision in that the picture is refreshed many times per second to give the impression of continuity. The picture cannot be transmitted as a whole; it has to be broken up into small elements. There were two fundamentally different ways of approaching this. George Carey of Boston, in 1875 proposed the transmission of every picture element simultaneously, each over a separate circuit. The alternate way – and the one subsequently adopted – was proposed independently in 1880 by W E Sawyer in the US and Maurice Leblanc in France. Their proposal was that each element of the picture was rapidly and systematically scanned, line by line, frame by frame. This established the possibility of using only a single wire, or channel, for transmission.

In 1873 the photoconductive properties of the element selenium were discovered: its electrical conduction varies with the amount of illumination falling on it. This discovery led to the 1884 patent of Paul Nipkow in Germany for a spirally-apertured rotating disc that provided at both sending and receiving ends a simple and effective method of image scanning. Until the advent of electronic scanning, all mechanical systems were related to Nipkow's disc.

The electrical response of selenium was relatively slow and just before the outbreak of the First World War German researchers invented a cell coated with potassium hydride possessing both an improved sensitivity and the ability to follow rapid changes of light. This discovery made possible a practical working system, especially since advances had been suggested for improving the receiving system.

In 1897 K F Braun in Germany introduced a cathode-ray tube with a fluorescent screen; its use as a picture receiver was suggested in 1907 by Boris Rosing in Russia.

By 1908 A A Campbell Swinton, a deferential Scot, felt able to put forward 'an idea only'. This idea involved the use of cathode-ray tubes magnetically deflected at both camera and receiver. In the camera was a mosaic screen of photoelectric elements. The image was focused on to this screen and discharged by a cathode-ray beam tracing out a line-by-line scanning sequence. Campbell Swinton's 'idea' was a little too ambitious for its time.

After the First World War another Scotsman, John Logie Baird, and C F Jenkins of America, both began experiments with Nipkow's mechanical system. In 1926 Baird gave the first demonstration of true television in that he electrically transmitted moving pictures. The reception was crude and ill-defined using as it did only 30 lines and repeating only ten times per second. Nevertheless it helped to stimulate research.

Swinton had pointed to the need for 100,000, and preferably 200,000, scannable elements in the picture, making 300 lines the minimum number. In 1923 V K Zworykin patented the iconoscope camera tube and further stimulated electronic scanning systems.

A regular television broadcasting service was begun in Germany in 1935, but the pictures were of medium definition only.

In Britain, EMI had set up a television research group in 1931 under Isaac Shoenberg. He proposed 405 lines and 50 frames per second. The standards were adopted in 1935 by the BBC who then began test transmissions from Alexandra Palace in London. The first notable outside broadcast was George VI's coronation in June 1937. The 20,000 or so viewers who had paid up to 60 guineas for their sets were mightily disappointed when transmission was summarily halted on 1 September 1939 when it appeared war was inevitable.

In America, NBC had publicly demonstrated their system on 30 April 1939 at the opening of the New York World Trade Fair. NBC, Columbia and Dumont networks all began broadcasting 1939 and 1940 and by mid-1940 there were 23 television stations in the US.

The war brought nearly all activity to an end – only six stations remained, but when in 1946 wartime restrictions were lifted in both America and Great Britain, there was a surge of interest and demand.

Above

Baird's apparatus for demonstrating the transmission of an outline.

Below

A photograph of a human face received by a Baird 'Televisor' in 1926. The sweeping lines of the rotating disc are clearly seen.

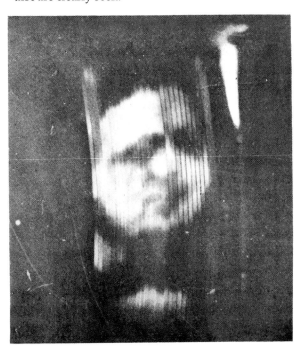

Colour television sets were available in America from 1950 but widespread purchase did not really take off until 1964.

A 1904 German patent contained the earliest proposals. Baird and H E Ives in America both gave mechanical demonstrations in 1928 and 1929 but of course the way ahead was with electronic systems. In 1938, just before war broke out, George Valensi of France pioneered the path to a colour transmission system compatible with existing black-and-white sets.

Today's plethora of networked and satellite television, together with the video recorder, provide a greater potential for passive entertainment in the home than could ever have been dreamed of even a few decades ago.

It has been a long and rapidly accelerating story of development from the days of shadow theatres, magic lanterns, zoetropes and their like. The home entertainment industry has all along reaped benefits arising from investigations into problems in more 'serious' spheres. Today, we are poised to benefit from holographs, interactive CDs, virtual reality, and so on. The direction popular home entertainment will take is wide open.

Despite spawning electricity, the 19th century was

Right **Building the *Practical Mechanics* Tele-Discovisor, 1933. Full instructions for constructing and setting up your own receiver at a cost of about £5.**

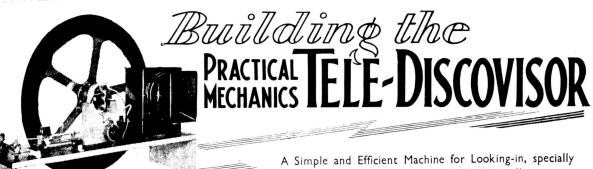

Building the PRACTICAL MECHANICS TELE-DISCOVISOR

A Simple and Efficient Machine for Looking-in, specially designed for " Practical Mechanics "

By H. J. BARTON CHAPPLE, Wh.Sch., B.Sc., A.M.I.E.E.

UNDOUBTEDLY the last few months have seen an enormous growth in the interest given to television, and many who viewed the event of this new science with avowed scepticism have become converted to "lookers." At the moment the B.B.C. are providing a television service on four nights in the week, the vision signals being broadcast from the London National station on 261 metres, and the accompanying sound from the Midland Regional station on 398 metres.

The design here described is of the simplest possible character, and admirable for initiating the newcomer into the mysteries of the art. There is not space here to deal with even the barest elements of the theory underlying television transmission and reception. So let me straightaway show every interested reader how he can make up his first assembly of television apparatus at a cost of about £5.

Materials Required

One Universal motor, complete with stand. (John Baker.)
One disc blank complete with boss. (Mervyn Sound and Vision Co., Ltd.)
One Seradex 150-ohm, 50-watt sliding resistance. (Trevor Pepper.)
Four Type B terminals marked A.C. mains (two), out + and input −. (Belling and Lee Ltd.)
Two terminal mounts. (Belling and Lee Ltd.)
One reconditioned lens box assembly, complete. (Baird Television Ltd.)
One used neon lamp with bakelite holder. (Baird Vision Ltd.)
One 255-ohm 60-watt Type Z2 Zenite resistance. (Smith Electric Co., Ltd.)
One interference filter unit, type 220/001. (Dubilier Condenser Co. (1925) Ltd.)
One 6-ohm filament rheostat complete with mounting bracket. (Peto-Scott Ltd.)
One wooden chassis. (Peto-Scott Ltd.)

This chassis can be obtained already fitted from the firm mentioned above, but for those readers desirous of making their own chassis, they can do so from the following details. It is ⅝ inch thick,

while the dimensions are 27 inches long by 9 inches wide. With the aid of a key-hole saw, cut a slot as shown, 17½ inches long by 1½ inches wide, with one edge of the slot 2⅝ inches from one long edge of the baseboard. This is to allow the 20-inch diameter disc to run freely when rotating at its normal speed of 750 revolutions per minute. Also to prevent the disc fouling the table it is necessary to raise the bottom of the baseboard 4½ inches by means of thick wooden sidepieces screwed to the underside.

A.C. OR D.C. MAINS APPLIED HERE.
SCANNING DISC
UNIVERSAL MOTOR
FIXED RESISTANCE
NEON LAMP
VARIABLE RESISTANCE
FILAMENT RHEOSTAT
INPUT +
INPUT −
LENS HOUSING
WOODEN CHASSIS

A perspective sketch of the Tele-Discovisor showing the universal motor finally decided on.

Marking Out

In the course of my experiments in building this apparatus I have tried out several different designs; in fact, the actual photographs accompanying this article indicate one form which I tried out. The finished product, however, as finally settled upon, is shown in the perspective line drawing, and it is this illustration to which the description refers.

It is necessary to pay particular attention to all the dimensions given in the drawings, at least in so far as the motor, neon lamp and lens assembly are concerned, for, unless

A.C. OR D.C. MAINS
TOP OF CHASSIS − 27" X 9"
9"
INPUT + INPUT −
2⅝"
SLOT IN CHASSIS
NEON LAMP HOLDER
2"
2¹¹⁄₁₆"
¾"
¾"
R
FIXED RESIST. 255 OHMS
TO EXISTING LEADS FROM MOTOR
LENS HOUSING
3⅛"
R1
R2
1⅝"
TO EARTH
2⅞" — 2⅞"
VAR. RESIST. 150 OHMS
BASE OF MOTOR
INTERFERENCE FILTER UNIT.
FIL. RHEOSTAT. 6 OHMS

Fig. 1.—The wiring diagram and layout of the components.

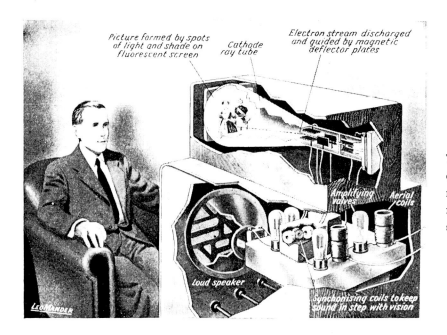

Picture formed by spots of light and shade on fluorescent screen

Cathode ray tube

Electron stream discharged and guided by magnetic deflector plates

Amplifying valves

Aerial coils

Loud speaker

Synchronising coils to keep sound in step with vision

The Emitron system, with electronic camera and cathode ray tube receiver soon replaced the Baird television system.

Microphone recording sound

Light and shade turned into waves of electrons and conveyed to amplifiers

Earphones from producer

Picture falling on mosaic screen and liberating electrons

Vacuum bulb

Window

Lens

Magnetic coils deflecting stream

Electrode

Cathode

Stream of electrons from cathode running over mosaic screen

Wire to power amplifiers and transmitters

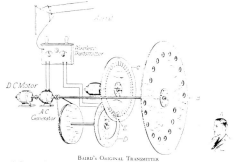

BAIRD'S ORIGINAL TRANSMITTER
A. Person to be transmitted. B. Revolving disc with lenses. C. Slotted disc revolving at high speed. D. Rotating spiral slot. E. Aperture through which light passes to light-sensitive cell.

Diagram of the Baird transmitter using a Nipkow disc. As each lens of disc (B) passes the image, the slotted disc (C) revolves once. Primitive 'interlacing' is achieved by means of the two offset spirals of lenses. The receiver projects a modulated light through two similar discs. One essential ingredient was mechanical synchronization.

nothing if not a mechanical age. It seemed as if nothing that moved could not be improved by some mechanical application – or at least by the application of newly-found scientific principles.

Music making

Singing and instrumental playing at home has a long history. As the 19th century progressed, music became invested with an enormous amount of significance, both moral and political; it was thought to be a sanitizing and refining influence. The 'Musical Evening' was an occasion common to high and low alike. Singers were most plentiful and, thanks to improved printing methods, an avalanche of sheet music appeared from the middle of the century. Ladies' magazines invariably included a song or two. The scope ranged from Stephen Foster (1826–64, of *Old folks at home* fame), topical moral ballads of hard-hitting sentimentality such as *Father's a Drunkard and Mother is dead* through the noble lines of Tennyson's *Maud* to copies of songs made popular on the stage and music hall (vaudeville). *Choral Harmony* and *The Amateur Musician* were but two of nearly 30 publications devoted to music in 1890.

The evidence from the Sears, Roebuck catalogue is that in the United States instrumental playing of all kinds was the most popular form of home entertainment in what was still basically a pioneering and settling country.

The piano, however, occupied pride of place, and benefited from several improvements in the early part of the 19th century. Pianos had wooden frames in the early 1800s and were consequently relatively fragile – Liszt played with such violence that he frequently required three instruments to complete a concert. An American, Alpheus Babcock of Boston, MA, cast the first iron frame in 1825. This enabled larger hammers to be used with heavier strings. Heinrich Steinweg – later Steinway – and his sons arrived in America in 1850 and developed and perfected the iron frame.

The musical glasses are tuned by pouring in water, and played with short rods of an undisclosed material. 'If the performer is gifted with a musical ear, he can obtain, by a little arrangement, a perfect Gamut by means of seven glasses which each give a note. A piece of music may be fairly rendered in this manner for the musical glasses frequently produce a very pure silvery sound.' The performance was clearly an occasion of the utmost gravity. How long the interest of the audience could be held is another matter.

A cats' musical evening, depicted by Louis Wain (1860–1939) in 1890. This drawing is a commentary both on the occasion and on the way of depicting it.

Despite the prestige associated with Broadwood's pianos in England, nearly 20,000 were imported annually for – in spite of Beethoven's endorsements of Broadwood's instruments – it was an article of faith that German pianos were the best. In Great Britain pianos weren't expensive. In 1911 *The Music Trades Record* advertised grands by Broadwood, Hagspiel and Bord at between £14 and £16 – so uprights and instruments of restricted range were affordable by many – especially 'on the 3-years' system' (instalment plan).

In America, wealthier homes had pianos imported from Europe, until home production of square pianos (a design originating in Germany, which may therefore reflect trends in immigration) took over in the 1830s. In 1867, in an article in *Atlantic Monthly* one James Panton enthused: 'almost every couple that sets up housekeeping on a respectable scale considers a piano only less indispensable than a kitchen range.'

Later in the century, upright pianos gained popularity, and by the 1890s manufacturers were left with an embarrassing quantity of square pianos taken in part exchange. These were disposed of in flamboyant style when in 1903 a 50-foot high pyramid of defunct square

A 'square' piano. The bass strings run the whole width of the instrument.

'The Gem roller organ is distinctly a musical instrument of excellent quality... it is so simply constructed that a child can operate it. The music is obtained from a roller which has teeth or pins like those of the cylinder of a regular Swiss music box. These pins operate on valve keys and the roller is turned by a gear which also works the bellows. The reeds used are the same as those used in regular cabinet parlor organs and the tone is therefore similar to that of a regular cabinet parlor organ.'

pianos was set alight on the Heights of Chelsea, Atlantic City.

Expertise was no longer confined to the finger-tips of the pianist, however, after the appearance of mechanical pianos. The 'Self-acting piano' of about 1820 used a horizontal cylinder similar to a barrel-organ which was set in motion by a spring. The Cylindichord used much the same idea.

A step forward was taken when, following the introduction of the pneumatically-operated lever as a substitute for the old tracker action in organ building, it was realised that perforated sheets of cardboard or rolls of paper could be used to control apparatus and so produce tunes. A patent for applying this idea was

43

The Autophone is hand operated; the fingers both pump the bellows and advance the perforated strip carrying the tune.

taken out in 1842 in France. In 1878 a table instrument with a handle was put on sale in New York – the Organette.

The next approach was to wheel an automaton up to the piano keyboard and let its pneumatically-operated fingers do the walking. In 1887 the Welte-Mignon Company in Germany patented a paper roll contrivance; at about the same time the Pianista was being manufactured in Paris. Here, a handle supplied the power, and the dynamic range of reproduction corresponded to the speed at which one turned the handle.

The Pianola was patented by the American E S Votey in 1897. It too was a 'push-up' contrivance. The notes were chosen by perforations on a roll passing over a 'tracker bar' which had holes corresponding to the notes of the keyboard (initially for 66, later for 88). The main control over dynamic force was by finesse in the foot-operated blowing, helped by hand levers.

Experienced 'players' could achieve great heights of sophistication which became even more impressive with the Reproducing Piano. This could repeat the complete performance of an artist, the roll having been mechanically produced from the artist's playing. Compositions for player pianos were undertaken by contemporary composers – taking advantage of the end of limitations to mere ten-fingered piano playing.

By 1901, all the trappings of a reproducing piano-

forte had been packed into the pianoforte itself. Between 1904 and 1930 two and a half million player pianos were sold in America; they never achieved quite the same popularity in Great Britain. Before the First World War, Duo-Art produced a player piano which could faithfully reproduce a performance by a specific pianist. These 'extraordinary mechanical contrivances' – described thus by Sir Alexander MacKenzie, Principal of the Royal Academy of Music – were taken seriously as sources of inspiration for budding artists because the piano sound was as yet imperfectly captured on gramophone discs. They were fun too, with much popular and jazz music being recorded on rolls, and an opportunity for the operator to influence the touch and the tempo.

Other mechanical instruments were available to those with sufficient interest and money. The barrel-piano worked on the same principle as a musical box, the pins on the revolving barrel striking against keyed teeth or actuating hammers. However, the sound was very jangly and hardly suitable for a drawing room. The self-playing violin, such as the Phonolist-Violina of 1910, comprised a player piano and three vertically mounted violins. This remained, not surprisingly, an expensive and little-seen curiosity.

In 1920 70 per cent of pianos manufactured in the US were player pianos, but by 1932 the combined inroads of radio, gramophone (phonograph) and Depression had made the instrument all but extinct.

Dolls

The sciences which are laid under contribution in the construction of toys are almost as multifarious as the arts which are employed in the manufacture of them ... for there is scarcely a species of manufacture or handicraft that does not contribute something to the amusement of the young.

Thus wrote Henry Mayhew in 1850 when there were some 1,866 toymakers and dealers in Great Britain. Dolls were no exception. Many were featured at the 1855 Industrial Exhibition in Paris.

Some were made in pliable contemporary materials such as gutta-percha or rubber. Hitherto, dolls' heads had been of wood, terra cotta or alabaster but from 1850 onwards Augusta Montanari and her son Richard were experimenting in Britain with wax heads. Dolls whose eyes, worked by counterweights, could open and close, had appeared earlier in the century.

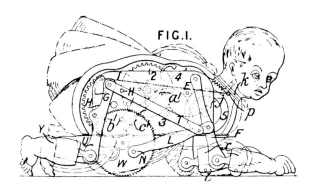

Newton's patent mechanical doll (No 2942 of 1871) 'is fitted with mechanism driven by clockwork, by which it is caused to imitate crawling, to move its head, and to produce inarticulate sounds.' A piece of stiff paper is intermittently brought into contact with the teeth of a wheel, 'thus producing inarticulate sounds, similar to those of a baby'.

The first talking doll was shown, along with many other advanced models, at an exhibition in 1855. It worked by a bellows mechanism patented by a Parisian mechanic in 1824. Raising one arm produced a 'Mama'; the other a 'Papa'.

Joints became moveable about this time, through a series of wires and strings inside the doll, an arrangement which continues to this day. Some readers may have experienced the trauma of trying to rehook a separated limb on to the strings inside the body.

In 1862, the famous French Jumeau family produced a doll made of bisque (unglazed porcelain). It had a swivel neck and its body was of kid stuffed with sawdust. Later Jumeau dolls had two or three faces so they could sleep, smile or cry at the turn of a knob on the head.

Autoperipatetikos was the wonderfully scientific name given to one of the first walking dolls which appeared in America in 1862. Many are still in working order – a testament to the robustness of their clockwork mechanism.

Thomas Edison had experimented with talking dolls and from late 1887 the Edison Toy Manufacturing Company was producing hand-driven phonograph dolls. In this field, however, the Frenchman Henri Lioret was a pioneer; his doll's phonograph was driven by a spring motor.

The buttons releasing the sweet cacophony of the farmyard are visible along the foredge of the book.

Books

Mechanics even invaded 'books'. According to one description: 'This book has represented on the left hand page the figure of some animal and on the right hand page there is some text descriptive of the creature exhibited. On pulling a small button attached to the book, the noise or sound peculiar to the animal will be emitted from under the opposite leaf.' In the illustration the pages have been removed to show the mechanism. So eat your heart out scratch-and-sniff books – there's nothing new under the sun.

Model railways

The single most exciting 'invention' of the 19th century in terms both of its popular perception and its all pervasivess was the railway. Model trains developed virtually in parallel with their full-grown reality. A simple engine with wagon appeared in the 1830s. Clockwork and simple steam locomotive engines appeared in the 1860s. The water-filled boilers were heated by methylated spirit burners and were variously called 'dribblers' or 'piddlers' – because they did.

Midland, Great Northern, and London & North Western Clockwork Trains.

As will be seen from the illustrations (which are from photographs of the actual models) these trains are mo
realistic in appearance. The mechanism and finish throughout is of the best, and the complete train with rai
is packed in a strong cardboard box.

No. SD. Gauge 0. L.N.W.R. Clockwork Trains, consisting of Scale Model George V. loco. and tender fitted with brake and reversing
gear, 1 Carriage, 1 guard's van with bogie wheels, complete with oval set of 16 wide radii rails. Len. 31 in. Carriage 10 d. Price with box ..

No. IAO. Gauge I. L.N.W.R. Passenger Express Train, consisting of Scale Model George V. loco. and tender, with brake
and reversing gear, 2 speeds, 1 carriage, 1 guard's van, complete with oval set of 20 wide radii rails. Length 58 in. Carriage paid. Price with box 5

No. GOA. Gauge 0. L.N.W.R. Passenger Express Loco., consisting of ditto engine and tender, with brake and reversing gear,
carriage and guard's van, mounted on bogie wheels, complete with oval track of 16 wide radii rails. Length 41 in. Carriage free 2

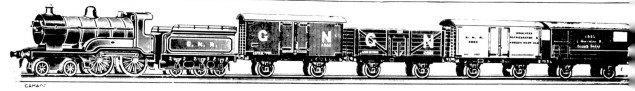

No. TZ. Gauge I. Scale Model G.N.R. Goods Train, consisting of loco. and tender, fitted with 2 speeds, brake and reversing gear,
1 open truck, 1 refrigerator van, 1 goods van, 1 goods guard's van, complete with oval set of 20 wide radii rails. Length 58 in. Carriage free.
Price with box 6

Gauge 0. 1¼ in.

Clockwork Train
16/6

Postage 10d.

No. SI. Consisting of Scale Model "George the Fifth" Loco. and Tender, with brake and reversing gear, 2 Carriages and Guard's Van with doors to ope
Oval Track of 16 wide radii rails.

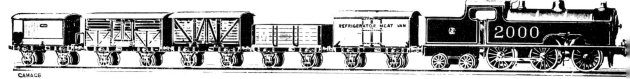

No. IL. Gauge I. Scale Model Midland Railway Goods Train, consisting of clockwork tank loco., fitted with 2 speeds reversing
gear and brake, all worked from cab, 1 open truck, 1 goods van, 1 refrigerator van, 1 cattle truck, 1 goods guard's van, complete with oval set of 20
wide radii rails. Length 58 in. Carriage free .. .. Price with box 5

No. GA. Gauge 0. Latest Type M.R. Co. Tank Loco., with correct English pattern trucks, as illustration, a really first-class train,
complete with oval of 16 wide radii rails. Length 38 in. .. Carriage free .. .. Price 2

No. GAY. Gauge 0. 1¼ in. Scale Model M.R. Goods Train, consisting of Locomotive and Tender with brake and reversing gear, Open Tru
1 Refrigerator Van, 1 Covered Goods Truck, 1 Cattle Truck, 1 Guard's Van, Oval Track of 12 Straight and 6 Curved Rails. Complete in Box
22/6 Carriage free.

A

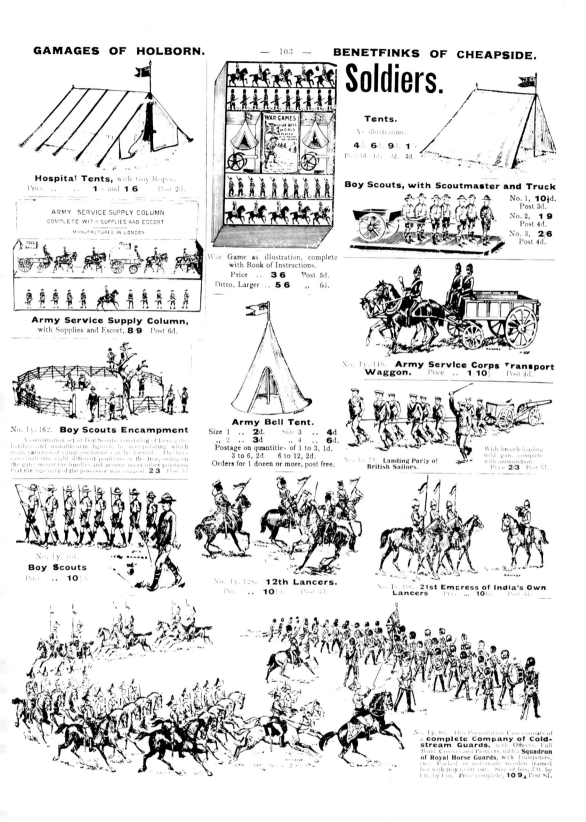

Soldiers.

Hospital Tents, with Guy Ropes.
Price .. .. **1** and **1 6**   Post 2d.

ARMY SERVICE SUPPLY COLUMN
COMPLETE WITH SUPPLIES AND ESCORT
MANUFACTURED IN LONDON

Army Service Supply Column,
with Supplies and Escort, **8 9**   Post 6d.

WAR GAMES FOR BOYS AND GIRLS PLAYED

War Game as illustration, complete
with Book of Instructions.
Price .. **3 6**   Post 5d.
Ditto, Larger .. **5 6**   ,, 6d.

No. Ty. 162. **Boy Scouts Encampment**
A combination set of Boy Scouts, consisting of tree, gate, hurdles and movable arm figures. In manipulating which many varieties of camp enclosure can be formed. The boys can climb into eight different positions in the tree, swing on the gate, mount the hurdles and assume many other positions that the ingenuity of the possessor may suggest. **2 3** Post 6d.

Army Bell Tent.
Size 1 .. **2d.**   Size 3 .. **4d**
,, 2 .. **3d**   ,, 4 .. **6d.**
Postage on quantities of 1 to 3, 1d.
3 to 6, 2d.   6 to 12, 2d.
Orders for 1 dozen or more, post free.

No. Ty. 164. **Boy Scouts**
Price .. **10**d.

No. Ty. 128. **12th Lancers.**
Price .. **10**d.   Post 3d.

Tents.
As illustration.
4d. **6**d. **9**d. **1 -**
Post 1d. 1d. 2d. 2d.

BOY SCOUTS, with Scoutmaster and Truck
No. 1, **10½d.**
Post 3d.
No. 2, **1 9**
Post 4d.
No. 3, **2 6**
Post 4d.

No. Ty. 116. **Army Service Corps Transport
Waggon.**   Price .. **1 10**   Post 4d.

No. Ty. 75. **Landing Party of
British Sailors.**
With breech-loading field gun, complete with ammunition.
Price **2/3** Post 3d.

No. Ty. 109. **21st Empress of India's Own
Lancers**   Price ... **10**d.   Post 3d.

No. Ty. 95. This Presentation Case consists of
a **complete Company of Cold-
stream Guards,** with Officers, Full
Band, Colours and Pioneers, with a **Squadron
of Royal Horse Guards,** with Trumpeters,
etc. Packed in well-made wooden framed
box with tray to lift out. Size of box, 2 ft. by
1 ft. by 1 in. Price complete, **10 9**. Post 9d.

Examples of toy soldiers (*above*) and trains (*left*) available from Gamages of Holborn, London in 1913.

The growing prosperity of the middle classes sought an outlet in realism and the German firms of Bing and Marklin, and the American firms of Ives and Lionel provided this, with whole sets of track, rolling stock, and accessories.

The first clockwork railway set which could be added to was exhibited at the Leipzig Toy Fair in 1891. It also established the beginnings of a gauge system for model railways. The British firm of Bassett-Lowke, established in 1899, developed a close relationship with Bing, and imported their products until the First World War put a damper on toy production. Antipathy to German goods died with the War, and in 1922 Bassett-Lowke introduced Bing's Miniature Table Railway, the smallest railway in the world. Demand was high because the houses of the interested public were small. The Bing-Bassett-Lowke association culminated in the Trix-Twin system, the most sophisticated system before the First World War, but it was soon challenged by Frank Hornby, whose Meccano was now well established, and who had more sophisticated selling techniques.

In 1938 Hornby produced his Dublo (ie double-0 gauge) electric system, which could fit on a table. In 1940 it was hailed as the ideal blackout hobby for boys and their fathers. The Second World War brought an end to the surge of enthusiasm for model trains, as it did to many other recreational activities. Things were never the same afterwards, and the firm of Hornby went into ignominious decline.

Tinplate had long been the material for cheap handmade (penny) toys, and the construction of metal toy trains was achieved relatively economically thanks to the many advances in factory and engineering techniques.

Soldiers

Flat soldiers were also of tin. Solid casting in lead alloy began to appear in France about 1790, though unsophisticated wooden soldiers survived in Great Britain and America until late in the 19th century when hollow casting in lead appeared, a process invented by Brittains about 1890. The metal alloy, containing antimony, is poured into a cool mould so that a skin forms around the outside of the shape. The antimony expands on cooling to give a crisp casting without the support of solid metal and the still-liquid metal in the centre of the mould is quickly poured out again, leaving a hollow figure.

On the road

Toy cars also mirrored the development of the automobile at the turn of the century. However, *their* locomotive power couldn't even be approximated and so chain, and later pedal, mechanisms, were used.

Patents for mechanical horses were applied for in 1822. One at least was mounted on three wheels and guided by handles on either side of the neck, which

Order No.
25.

Tandem Toy Automobile.

The flush-sided body is a really good model of the latest practice. Curved panels with ½-round beading. Specially well painted, lined and varnished and upholstered in sanitary leather. The chassis is fitted with ball bearings throughout, and is cycle made. Front axle will be appreciated by motorists. Fittings include speedometer, motor clock, two plated lamps and horn, wind-screen, adjustable seat, side doors, band brake, starting handle, finished any colour.

THE LAST WORD IN TOY AUTOS.

Ball-bearing pedals.

Pneumatic tyred wheels.   Price **£11 9 6**

Carriage extra on all above motors outside our London Carrier radius

K..

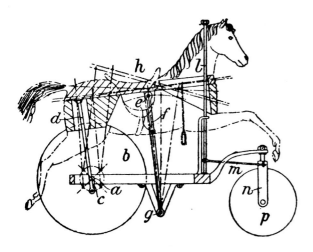

Brooman's patent hobby horse (No 1076 of 1862) has three wheels and is arranged so that the rider may imitate galloping. 'Motion is effected by the rider jumping alternately into the stirrups and the saddle (h) while grasping a rod (l).' It is also suggested that 'by means of clockwork or other mechanism the horse may be made to move automatically for a certain time.'

controlled various mechanical appliances inside the animal's body. It sounds very like an embryonic bicycle.

Rocking horses have long been popular. Originally, the horse's body stood on a pair of rockers; the swing-bar type was patented in America in 1884.

Fretwork

The fretsaw dates back to the 16th century and resulted from the development of steels for spring-driven clocks. Serrated, a fine steel clock spring provided a narrow blade. Arranged on a frame to move up and down, it was used to cut fine woods and veneers for furniture.

This is the so-called 'jig-saw' which, in the 1760s, was used by print makers such as John Spilsbury of London to dissect maps glued to wood as an aid to teaching geography. Jigsaw puzzles have continued as teaching aids ever since.

Other subjects became popular from the end of the 18th century – panoramas, architectural and domestic scenes much as we find today. The borders were generally interlocking, but the centres were not; fully

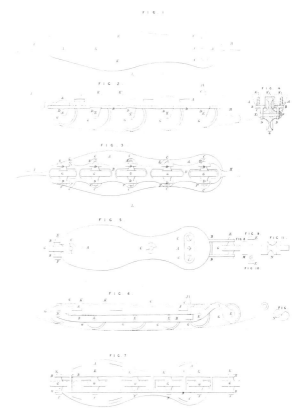

Robert Tyers' patent for roller skates (No 4782 of 1823). This apparatus is 'to be attached to boots, shoes and other covering for the purpose of travelling or pleasure.'

As the advertising copywriter explained: 'The art of skating on wheels remains popular and will always be worth the attention of those who are really fond of exercise whatever the season of the year or state of the thermometer. The young skater should secure the services of a skilful instructor, and implicitly follow his advice.'

Fretwork Machines. Of British Manufacture Throughout.

No. 1. Briton Fretsaw .. 14/6
No. 2. Ditto, with Nickel Plated Tilting Table and Emery Wheel 17/-

The "BRITON" Machine is one of the cheapest reliable Treadle Fretsaws on the market. The arms will take 18 in. work, and the height to the Table is 32 in. The Machine is fitted with Hobbies Patent Lever Steel Clamps with new patent screws and shackles. There is also an improved Dust Blower, and the end of the Balance-Wheel Spindle is pierced for holding a Drill. A Drill Bit, Wrench, Oil Can, Saws, and two Designs are sent out with each Machine.

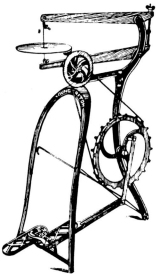

Young Briton, 13/6

The Young Briton is a new model this season and is a cheap and reliable Fretsaw. The frame of the Machine is made entirely of iron finished in cycle enamel. The Balance-Wheel Pulley and Table are the same as used on our "Briton" Machine. The Saw Clamps are our Patent Spring Open pattern. A Wrench, one dozen Saws and Design are sent with each mnchine.

The "Companion" Lathe and Fretsaw.

This "Companion" Machine forms a useful Amateur's Lathe and Fretsaw. The large Driving Wheel has tw of varying depths to give a change of speed. The Lathe head is provided with a 2-in. Face Plate, a Spur Cen a Screw Centre for turning Cups It has also a solid Emery Wheel and a Drill Spindle. The Tail Stock has Feed Centre. The Lathe is provided with two Rests. three Turning Tools, Wrench and Screwdriver, and Fretsawing Attachment, Designs, Saws, Drill Points. &c. Swing of Lathe, 5 in. Length of Bed 24 in. between Centres, 14 in. A Circular Saw Attachment with Nickel-plated and polished Table can be fitte "Companion" Lathe. The Fretsawing Attachment is secured to the Lathe Bed by one bolt, and ca on and taken off at leisure. It is fitted with 19-in. arms, with Trusses to prevent bending, Dust Blower. nicke Tilting Table, and Hobbies Patent Lever Saw Clamps.
Lathe and Fretsaw. **35/-** Lathe and Tools. **27/6** Fretsaw Attachment. **8/6** Circular Saw Attachm

No. 1. A1 Treadle Fretsaw.
No. 2. With Nickle-Plated Table Emery Wheel ..

Considering its low price of one guine Hobbies A1 Fretsaw is acknowledged to surpassed. The Machine is fitted wit Hobbies Patent Lever Clamps. Thes securely grip the finest Saw Blades, and th so made that the Lever cannot fly back and the tension of the Saw.

The end of Balance-Wheel Spindle is an to hold a Drill, and there is also an im Dust Blower.

A Drill Bit, Oil Can, Screwdriver, Spann dozen Saws, and two Designs are sent wit Machine.

TREADLE CIRCULAR SAW.

This neat little Treadle Circular Saw has been specially designed by us at the urgent re quest of a number of customers. It takes a 4-in. Saw and is pro vided with a Sliding Table moving parallel with the Saw on ac curately machined V Slides. This Table is machine graduated, and has an adjustable fence which can be set to any angle, thus en abling wood to be cut to any desired angle. This tool is splendidly suited for geometrical inlaying, as by its use any number of Squares, Triangles, Rhombus or Rhomboids, may be cut identical in size and accurate in shape. Most delightful pat terns can thus be formed from different coloured varieties of wood. Examples of Geometrical Inlay work cut with Hobbies Treadle Circular Saw.
Price .. **22/6**
Carriage forward.

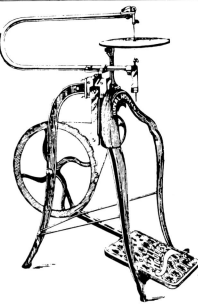

Royal Hobbies Fretsaw.

No. 1 As illustrated, with Dulled Nickelled Table and Japanned Saw Frame **32/-**
Ditto, with Plated Table **34/-**
No. 2, With all Bright Parts Plated, including Table and Saw Frame 933. **37/-**

All Machines are carefully tested before being despatched, packed in cra complete working order, and ready for immediate use. Direct from Wo Machines are sent by Rai at the Railway Company's risk. The purchase carriage on delivery.

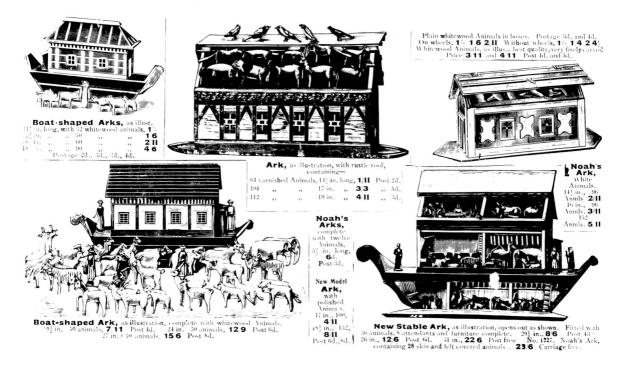

Boat-shaped Arks, as illust.
1½ in. long, with 52 whitewood animals, **1/-**
16 in., „ 50 „ **16**
16½ in., „ 60 „ **2 11**
18 „ „ 90 „ **4 6**
Postage 2d., 3d., 3d., 4d.

Ark, as illustration, with rustic roof,
containing—
64 varnished Animals, 14½ in. long, **1/11** Post 2d.
104 „ „ 17 in. „ **3 3** „ 5d.
112 „ „ 19 in. „ **4 11** „ 5d.

Noah's Arks, complete with twelve Animals, 5½ in. long, **6d.** Post 3d.

New Model Ark, with polished Animals, 17 in., 100, **4 11** 18½ in., 152, **8 11** Post 6d., 8d.

Plain whitewood Animals in boxes. Postage 3d. and 4d.
On wheels, **1/- 1 6 2 11** Without wheels, **1/- 1 4 2 4½**
Whitewood Animals, as illus., best quality, very finely carved.
Price **3 11** and **4 11** Post 4d. and 5d.

Noah's Ark, White Animals.
14½ in., 96 Anmls. **2 11**
16 in., 96 Anmls. **3 11**
152 Anmls. **5 11**

Boat-shaped Ark, as illustration, complete with whitewood Animals.
19½ in. 50 animals, **7 11** Post 4d. 24 in. 50 animals, **12 9** Post 6d.
27 in. 150 animals, **15 6** Post 8d.

New Stable Ark, as illustration, opens out as shown. Fitted with
36 animals, 8 attendants and furniture complete. 20½ in., **8 6** Post 4d.
26 in., **12 6** Post 6d. 51 in., **22 6** Post free No. 1227. Noah's Ark,
containing 28 skin and felt covered animals ... **23 6** Carriage free.

Gamage's Noah's arks.

Left Hobbies 'Combination' lathe and fretsaw – 35 shillings. Fretwork was a craft which became a hobby encouraged by such organizations as 'The Cottage Arts Association', which was anxious 'to combat the torrent of machine-wrought sameness.'

interlocking puzzles were introduced at the beginning of the 20th century. 'Jigsaws', as the puzzles are now called, have had various bouts of popularity, notably during the Depression and after the Second World War.

The fretsaw has uses other than making puzzles, and has remained extremely popular among domestic handymen who, having subdued the urge to saw out copious quantities of decorative carvings, now use the tool sparingly and to good effect.

Answer to puzzle page 18
The Divided Farm
How the fences were put up when the old man's wishes had been carried out.

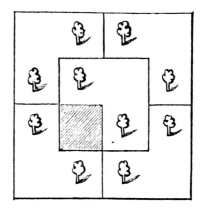

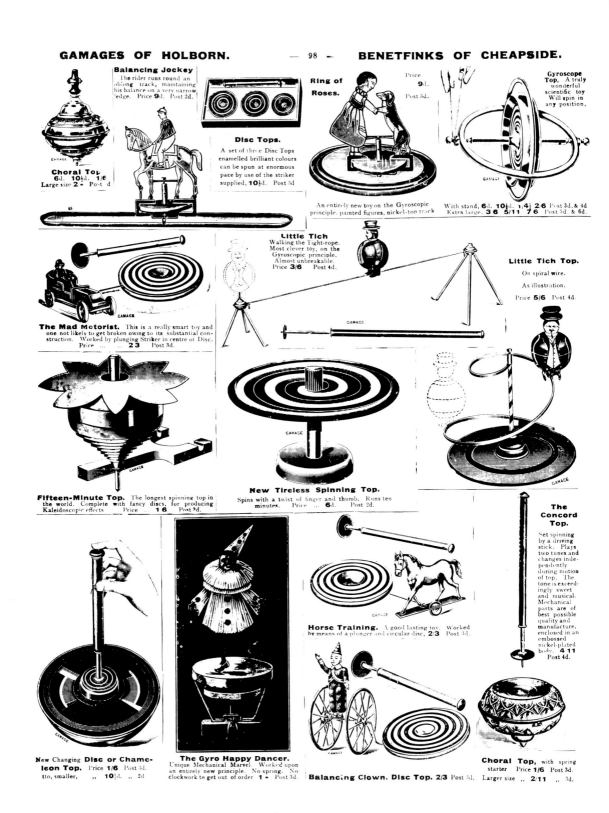

Balancing Jockey
The rider runs round an oblong track, maintaining his balance on a very narrow 'edge. Price **9**d. Post 2d.

Choral Top.
6d. **10½**d. **1/6**
Large size **2 -** Post d

Disc Tops.
A set of three Disc Tops enamelled brilliant colours can be spun at enormous pace by use of the striker supplied, **10½**d. Post 3d

Ring of Roses.
Price **9**d.
Post 3d.
An entirely new toy on the Gyroscopic principle. painted figures, nickel-top track

Gyroscope Top. A truly wonderful scientific toy Will spin in any position.
With stand, 6d. **10½**d. **1/4 2/6** Post 3d. & 4d.
Extra large. **3 6 5/11 7 6** Post 5d. & 6d.

The Mad Motorist. This is a really smart toy and one not likely to get broken owing to its substantial construction. Worked by plunging Striker in centre of Disc.
Price ... ... **2 3** Post 3d.

Little Tich
Walking the Tight-rope. Most clever toy, on the Gyroscopic principle. Almost unbreakable.
Price **3/6** Post 4d.

Little Tich Top.
On spiral wire.
As illustration.
Price **5/6** Post 4d.

Fifteen-Minute Top. The longest spinning top in the world. Complete with fancy discs, for producing Kaleidoscopic effects Price ... **1 6** Post 3d.

New Tireless Spinning Top.
Spins with a twist of finger and thumb. Runs ten minutes. Price ... **6**d. Post 2d.

The Concord Top.
Set spinning by a driving stick. Plays two tunes and changes independently during motion of top. The tone is exceedingly sweet and musical. Mechanical parts are of best possible quality and manufacture, enclosed in an embossed nickel-plated body. **4 11** Post 4d.

Horse Training. A good lasting toy. Worked by means of a plunger and circular disc, **2/3** Post 3d.

New Changing Disc or Chameleon Top. Price **1/6** Post 3d.
tto, smaller, ,, **10**d. ,, 2d

The Gyro Happy Dancer.
Unique Mechanical Marvel. Worked upon an entirely new principle. No spring. No clockwork to get out of order **1 -** Post 3d.

Balancing Clown. Disc Top. 2/3 Post 3d.

Choral Top, with spring starter Price **1/6** Post 3d.
Larger size ,, **2/11** ,, 3d.

Gamage's tops

Philosophical toys

There is a tendency in this country, we fear, to fall into the error of construction toys for boys that are not only too expensive for the general purse, but too scientific and elaborate – model locomotives which go by steam, working pumps, model steam vessels, mice running by machinery, and for the girls dolls that move along the table, raise their arms and cry Papa and Mama. This is carrying machinery into the nursery with a vengeance. It may be very well calculated to foster the mechanical spirit, but not to relax the mind, the proper object of toys. They are far too expensive ever to come into general use, so their influence is not likely to be great.
Cassell's Magazine, 1867

'Philosophical' toys were those small enough to demonstrate the principles of science – or 'natural philosophy' – on a table top. Fitting tidily into an ordered life, they were popular in Victorian drawing rooms with parents and children alike.

Many such toys worked by means of magnetic needles, for example floating tortoises, fishes, and ducks drawn along by a magnet. In Nuremberg, the German toymaker Freischermann developed the idea with notable commercial success.

Similarly demonstrating scientific principles, cam-phor boats showed the effects of surface tension, while other vessels were driven by pieces of chalk reacting with vinegar added to the water. In 1891 Thomas Piot, of London, patented his steam pulse jets which he used to power small boats – some only two inches long – known as 'pop-pop boats'.

The earnest Victorian mind thought nothing could be more respectable than to become usefully informed. Combine that with the thrill of entering into the hurly burly world of modern engineering and science and what more could one want?

Mechanical toys

Clockwork was of course a well-established driving force and was simply and imaginatively applied to a range of toys. Not only were there obviously moving objects such as cars and locomotives, but more subtle automata.

Automata were interesting for scientific and mechanical investigation. They certainly weren't new, having existed at least in ancient Egyptian times. Later, a contemporary of the Emperor Hadrian (76–138) tells

'The road locomotive, illustrating the principles of inertia and motive power' – using what we would now call a friction motor.

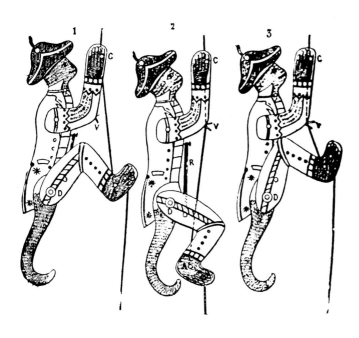

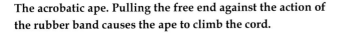

The acrobatic ape. Pulling the free end against the action of the rubber band causes the ape to climb the cord.

Automatic puppets. Each of the hollow tubes contains a marble, or a blob of mercury, which runs back and forth, causing the model to descend the stairs.

of a wooden dove which flew. The body was apparently filled with air which caused movement as it slowly escaped. The church stepped early into the working-model market. Figures of saints and madonnas might need to move but anyone constructing a model so cleverly that its workings were incomprehensible was liable to stand accused as a mechanician or necromancer.

In the 16th century Bernardias Baldi, an Italian mathematician, built human figures which moved ingeniously on hydraulic principles. By the end of the 18th century, the principle of counter-balance was being used, for example to open and close dolls' eyes.

Electrical toys

'It will now perhaps interest our readers to describe a charming little plaything which is a great favourite with children and as well has the incontestable merit of early initiating them into all the principal phenomena of the statics of electricity teaching them the science of physics in an amusing form'. So wrote the editor of *Popular Scientific Recreations* introducing 'a small electrophorus invented by M J Peiffer' (*illustrated right above*).

Electricity was of course extremely exciting stuff to be dabbling with. The figures in the illustration (*right, below*) were intended for ordinary use as scarf pins or ornaments, but seem more akin to the squirting flowers clowns wear than pieces of serious jewellery. *The Magic Lantern Journal* promoted 'popular science for Lecture Room and Domestic Circles' and was well able to advise on the construction of an 'electrical machine.'

Cassell's *Book of Outdoor Sports and Indoor Amusements* (1880) instructed the intrepid amateur scientist with the odd cork, flask, tube *etc* to hand 'How to make an electroscope', 'How to blow out a candle with an electrical wind', and 'How to give a shock to several people'. Thus guided through all manner of experiments, a boy was able to appreciate the unfolding of the wonderful world of science; for such topics undoubtedly were a boy's preserve – and a 'fast' boy at that, according, ironically, to one *Cassell's Magazine* contributor (in 1867): 'The toy shops, following the mechanical genius of the country, seem bent upon converting the steam engine into a plaything. If Watt had been told half a century ago that his grand invention

'The electrophorus consists of a thin sheet of ebonite and a tinned wooden disc. Place it flat on a wooden table, and thoroughly rub it with the hand; if it is then lifted and the sheet of tin lightly touched, a spark is elicited up to half an inch in length. The electrophorus is completed by the addition of a number of small dolls placed on it to exhibit in a very amusing manner the phenomena of attraction and repulsion.'

Electricity makes the gold rabbit tap on a bell, a diamond bird flap its wings, or the death's head gnash its teeth and roll its eyes 'and by so doing cause much surprise among the spectators'.

Electric Generating Station.

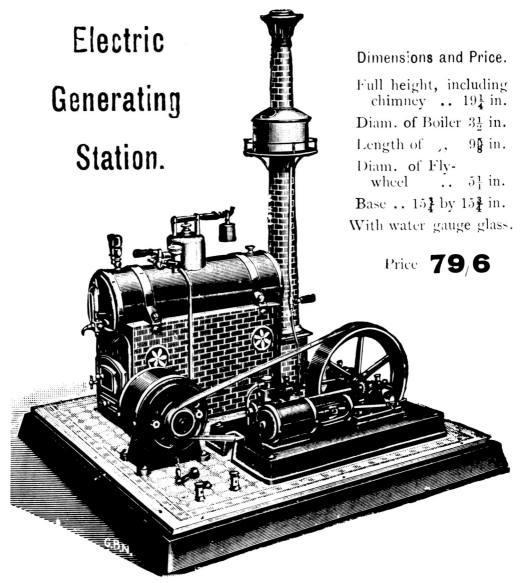

Dimensions and Price.

Full height, including
    chimney .. 19¼ in.
Diam. of Boiler 3½ in.
Length of ,, 9⅝ in.
Diam. of Fly-
    wheel .. 5¼ in.
Base .. 15¾ by 15¾ in.
With water gauge glass.

Price **79/6**

With powerful Engine with improved slide valve cylinders, oxydised brass boiler with complete fittings, correct steam pressure gauge, dynamo in superior finish, mechanical parts of the engine all finely polished, base, etc., mat black japanned, with driving belt connecting engine and dynamo, with switch and pole clamps for conducting the electric current produced by the dynamo. All fittings highly nickelled. Boiler house and chimney stamped (imitation brickwork), with feed pump, three-way cock, lever safety valve, bell steam whistle, steam jet oiler, steam dome, fire door, vapour spirit lamp, with heater for feed water on chimney, exhaust steam passes through chimney. Mounted on strong wooden base with finely japanned metal plate.

Above
A double-engine at $3.50.

Left
Electric Generating Station at 79 shillings and sixpence .

Before we all had to be protected from ourselves, chemicals with which to carry out experiments were readily available.

Pharaoh's serpent, an indoor firework, is made by 'pouring sulpho-cyanide of potassium into a solution of nitrate acid on mercury. The white combustible powder is filtered, transformed into a stiff pulp by means of water containing a solution of gum, nitrate of potash is added, and the pulp is shaped into cones which are allowed to dry thoroughly. When lit, the sulpho-cyanide slowly expands and five-and-twenty inches of "serpent" emerge. The residue comprises cyanide of mercury and cyanogen; it is very poisonous [!] and should be thrown away. It is to be regretted that Pharaoh's serpent should herald his appearance by the disagreeable, suffocating odour of sulphurous acid.'

would have been converted into a toy for the delectation of boys, how he would have stared – a real working engine for five and sixpence.' It was forgotten, perhaps, that it was a model of a Newcomen engine that inspired Watt to make his original experiments.

Possibly because the results of working steam engines were much more 'known' phenomena than the results of electrical activity, such engines became very popular in the late Victorian and Edwardian periods. German examples were particularly imaginative, their attention to detail making them more realistic.

Chemistry sets

The illustrations in this section show a number of chemical experiments which had immense appeal to the scientific mind. The fact that results are predictable, repeatable and explicable should be of great support to the ordered universe.

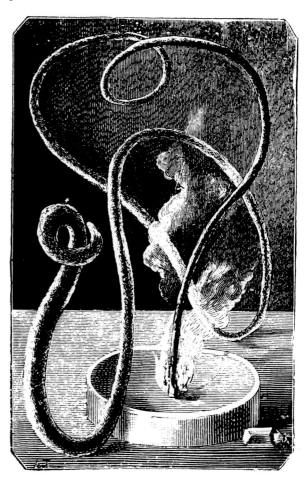

Exposing periwinkles to the vapours of sulphurous acid whitens them instantaneously while (*below*) columbines plunged into a mixture of 10 parts common ether and one part liquid ammonia take instantaneously a bright green tint.

However, the basic chemistry set contained simple materials (such as calcium carbonate, sulphur, iron filings, and copper sulphate), a few test tubes and a spirit lamp, but (like many kits boxed for children) never lived up to the picture on the lid. Pharaoh's serpent, whose raw materials and products of combustion are potentially lethal, is in a different league.

Constructional toys

In 1901, tin boxes containing some strips of perforated metal, nuts and bolts, and costing 7s 6d came on to the market. On the lid it said: 'Mechanics Made Easy'. This was the brainwave of Frank Hornby, a meat importer's clerk from Liverpool. The system soon came to be known as Meccano.

Constructional toys, of which Meccano was the most sophisticated and diverse in its potential, had appeared since the end of the 18th century. At first, they consisted of sets of simple wooden blocks of varying size and shape, which could be assembled into buildings, farmsteads or even whole villages. The earliest came from Germany, were cheap and colourful, and contained people and animals. Some could make walled towns; others castle walls. In the Museum of the City of New York is an example of a set (1850) from which could be built a log cabin. American toymakers used lithographed paper to decorate their blocks – even producing 'stained glass' windows for church sets to build on Sundays.

Despite the relative visual realism and versatility of these sets, one of the drawbacks for the serious constructor was that they needed to rest and balance one on top of another. In 1867, the American Jesse Charles Crandall patented an interlocking system composed of tongued and grooved blocks. Simple blocks still featured in the Gamage's 1913 catalogue alongside the more sophisticated 'Kliptiko' (a construction system of metal tubes) and Gamage's own Interlocking Bricks.

This system retained its popularity until the 1930s, when we find such building materials as Lott's Bricks (made of real stone) or Bako, whose Bakelite building elements, threaded on vertical wires, would provide, for example, a 1930s suburban house complete with curved bay windows. 'Minibrix' introduced moulded studs on their rubber blocks, a feature taken up and refined in plastic by the now phenomenally successful Danish firm of Lego in 1955.

Frank Hornby's patent (No 587 of 1901) for an improved toy or educational device for children and young people – otherwise known as Meccano. The idea was to construct mechanical objects, buildings etc from independent pieces. That Hornby was disposed towards railways is apparent from his claim that 'the pieces serve for the construction of bridges, tunnels, stations, signals, signal boxes, hoists and buildings in general, as well as cranes and railway lines as shown in the illustration.'

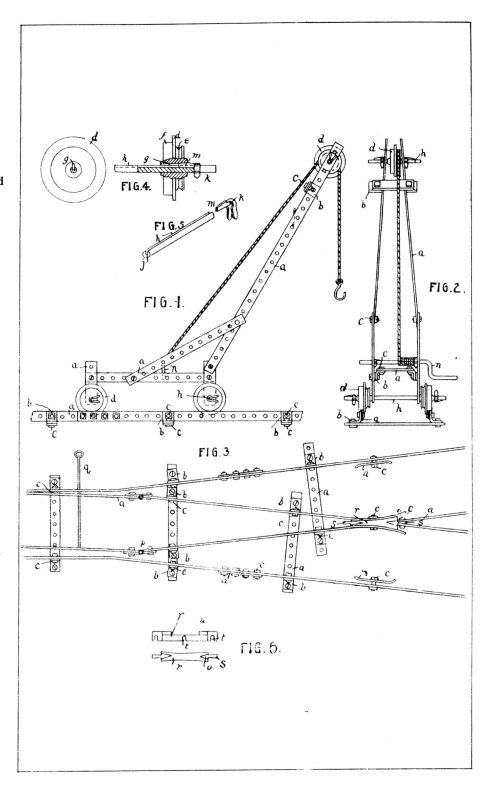

FIG.4.

FIG.5.

FIG.1.

FIG.2.

FIG.3.

FIG.5.

Wooden Constructional Toys.

HOW TO BUILD "DREADNOUGHTS" THAT FLOAT. (Patent applied for No. 12653 12.)

A VALUABLE IMPROVEMENT ON OUR WELL-KNOWN DREADNOUGHT SHIPBUILDING BLOCKS.

All ships are fitted with a special keel which enables them to **float upright in water.**

These Shipbuilding Blocks are undoubtedly amongst the finest Toys on the Market. Each Box contains Wood Blocks, Guns, Flags, &c., with instructions for building Warships, type: H.M.S. "Dreadnought," H.M.S. "Lord Nelson," H.M.S. "King Edward VII." etc., as well as Cruisers, type: H.M.S. "Invincible," etc., Torpedo Boats, Forts, etc. This Toy is not only very entertaining, but most instructive.

	No. 1	1½	2	3
	1 10½	**2 11**	**6 6**	**10 6**
Postage	4d.	5d.	8d.	10d.

INTERLOCKING BUILDING BRICKS.

Fort.
Built with Gamage's Interlocking Bricks.

Bridge.
Built with Gamage's Interlocking Bricks.

House.
Built with Gamage's Interlocking Bricks.

The Gamage Interlocking Building Bricks, without question, are far and away the best bricks ever invented for children. Their chief feature is, of course, the notches or slots into which the bricks interlock, so that when a model has been constructed, whether it be a House, Fort, or Windmill, it can be carried about and played with as if it were nailed or glued together. Even apart from the interlocking arrangement the shapes and sizes have been so arranged that the number of different models which can be made from a single box, is quite extraordinary. The Bricks are of Best Beech Hardwood, machined and planed to gauge, so that any brick (no matter what size) will interlock with another and will not come apart until required.

An illustrated Booklet is supplied with each Box, showing how to construct

Model Bridges, Churches, Windmills, Houses, Forts, Monuments, &c., &c.

| No. 1. | **10½d.** | Post 3d. | | No. 1½. | **1 9** | Post 4d. | | No. 2. | **2 4½** | Post 5d. | | No. 2½. | **3 11** | Post 9d. |

A DELIGHTFUL & FASCINATING TOY

Consisting of wood Blocks, wheels, axles pulleys, rods, pins and tongues with tools and manual of illustrated instructions for constructing

Cranes, Motor Cars, Engines, and all sorts of Models that work.

All Models when made are Strong and Rigid Toys for Practical use.

Pin-Tung   Or Model Making Made Easy.

Trip Hammer.

Open Motor Car.

All Models can be taken to pieces and used over and over again.

The Tower Bridge. A correct Model.

2/6	Box makes	11	Models.	Post	4d.
3 6	,,	23	,,	,,	5d.
5 6	,,	28	,,	,,	6d.
8/6	,,	40	,,	,,	8d.
12 6	,,	46	,,	,,	10d.
17/6	,,	50	,,	,,	1/-
21/-	,,	53	,,	,,	1/-

I

Constructional Toys.

Model Steamers.

Exceptionally well made.

Packed in box with Hull assembled.

Mast and Riggings separate.

Easy to put together or take apart.

Travel on Wheels.

No. 1. 12 in. long. **2 11** ea. Post 4d.

No. 2. 17½ in. long, **4 11** Post 5d.

No. 3. 2 ft. 4 in. long, **6 11** Post 6d.

Battleship Building Bricks. Beautifully carved in hardwood and enamelled in colours for building different model battleships. Made to float. Box to hold 3 boats, **8 6** Post 6d. Ditto 4 boats, **12 6** Post 8d. Ditto 6 boats, **18 6** Post 10d

"KLIPTIKO."

"Kliptiko" is simple enough to joyfully interest a young child, while its possibilities are expansive enough to prevent that interest from flagging as the child grows up.

The Young Engine Builder. Price **10½**d. Post 3d. **1/10½** Post 3d. **2 11½** Post 4d. **3/11** Post 4d. **4/11** Post 5d. **7/11** Post 6d.

THERE IS NO LIMIT TO WHAT CAN BE MADE.

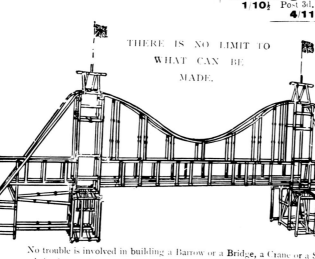

No trouble is involved in building a Barrow or a Bridge, a Crane or a Symmetrical and graceful Tower. There are no irritating small parts to get into the wrong place, or in the reverse position to that which that they should be. All Constructions are quite rigid and steady, and working models may be operated without slackness or fear of collapse. The Standard Units are the same in each set, making all pieces interchangeable, and allowing one set to be added to another of a lesser or a greater price. No. 1 **10½**d. Post 3d. No. 2 **2/4½** Post 4d. No. 3 **4/11** Post 5d. No. 4 **9/11** Post 6d.

The Young Motor Maker.

Complete set of parts in wood to make a Motor Van.

10½d. **1/10½** **2/6** Post 4d. 5d.

Fire Escape.

A complete set of materials and instructions for building above.

Price **2/6** Post 3d.

The ultimate in malleability: William Harbutt's Plasticine was introduced in 1897. Plasticine comes in a whole range of colours, and mice made from it, it seems, will cause the maid to leap on to a chair, dropping the tea tray in fright.

From the start, Meccano sets contained wheels so at last structures could be built that would move. The Meccano *Inventor's Outfit* appeared in 1920; it included bevel gears, threaded cranks, gear wheels, racks, pinions, worms, hinges, braced girder strips and so on. The engineering industry was at a peak and now boys of all ages could be part of that industry.

Meccano Magazine was launched in 1916, and the Meccano Club emerged after the First World War. As well as offering ideas, sharing members' models, and speaking on matters of general engineering interest, the Club fostered identification not only with one product but also all that was great, good and ambitious in the nation. As Basil Harley writes in *Constructional Toys* 'a Meccano Guild Certificate read like a top grade school report.'

Meccano never regained its pre-eminence after the Second World War, during which production of toys and leisure objects in Britain all but ceased. More recently, systems based on mechanics have had a hard battle to fight against those based on electronics. Our contention is that the success of a nation's manufacturing industry must be founded on children inspired by Meccano, rather than by Nintendo.

Punch cartoon, 1902

Hostess. "I thought you were going to play 'Bridge'!"
Host. "So we are, but they are playing 'Ping-pong' in the dining-room, and 'fires' in the billiard-room, Jack's trying to imitate Dan Leno in the drawing-room, and Dick's got that infernal gramophone of his going in the hall, and they are laying supper in the smoking-room, so *we're* going to the nursery!"

Chronology

Further reading

Carol Adams
Ordinary Lives
Virago, 1982

Peter Bailey
Leisure and Class in Victorian England
Routledge & Kegan Paul, 1978

Eric Barnoun
A History of Broadcasting in the United States 3 vols.
OUP New York, 1966–1970

R C Bell
Board and Table Games
Shire Publications, 1981

Geoffrey Best
Mid-Victorian Britain
Fontana Press, 1979

Donna R Braden
Leisure and Entertainment in America
Henry Ford Museum, 1988

K Char
Talking Machines
London HMSO, 1981

Rodney Dale and Joan Gray
Edwardian Inventions
W H Allen, 1979

Eric J Evans
The Forging of the Modern State
Longman, 1983

Roland Gelatt
The Fabulous Phonograph 1877–1977
Macmillan, 1977

J D Hart
The Popular Book: A History of America's Literary Tastes
OUP New York, 1950

Cynthia A Hoover
Music Machines American Style
Washington D.C.: Smithsonian Institution Press, 1971

H Thomas Inge
Handbook of American Popular Culture
Greenwood Press, 1980

Mrs F Neville Jackson
Toys of Other Days
London, 1948

S Kaplan
Leisure in America: A Social Inquiry
J Wiley & Sons, 1960

Tom Lewis
Empire of the Air: The Creation of Radio
Harper Collins, 1991

R W Malcolmson
Popular Recreations in English Society 1700–1850
CUP, 1973

Oliver Read and Walter L Welch
From Tin Foil to Stereo: Evolution of the Phonograph
Indianapolis, Howard W Sams, 1959

Robert Roberts
The Classic Slum
Harmondsworth, 1971

E P Thompson and Eileen Yeo
The Unknown Mayhew
Harmondsworth, 1973

J K Walton and J Walvin
Leisure in Britain 1780–1939
Manchester U P, 1983

W Weber
Music and the Middle Class
London, 1975

Index

Illustration on facing page
Whitmore's patent (no 3,371
of 1810) for a magnetic toy 'to
facilitate the teaching of
children to spell, read and
cypher in any tongue.'
By manipulating the strings,
the teacher causes the figure
of a horse to turn, nod its
head, pick up a letter with its
magnetic mouth, and lay the
letter on a rack, thus building
up a letter 'in any tongue' –
provided it uses the Roman
Alphabet.